The FRIENDSHIP BOOK

of Francis Gay

D. C. THOMSON & CO. LTD.
London Glasgow Manchester Dundee

A Thought
For Each Day
In 1983

" Everything that is done in the world is done by hope." Martin Luther.

SOLITUDE

There is peace by lonely waters,
There is calm in stilly woods,
When good fortune finds us sharing
One of Nature's quieter moods;
And it's there our worries vanish,
No worldly care intrudes.

JANUARY

SATURDAY—JANUARY 1.

MOST of us are familiar with Tennyson's lines about the New Year:

Ring out the old, ring in the new . . .
Ring out the false, ring in the true.

Is there anything more cheerful than the sound of bells on the night air? In England bells used to be muffled on New Year's Eve so that when they were rung before midnight, the sound was weak, but after midnight they rang out loud and clear.

It would be a good idea today to " muffle " any thoughts of the past which may sadden or dismay us, and to greet 1984 with hope and joy.

SUNDAY—JANUARY 2.

TAKE therefore no thought for the morrow: for the morrow shall take thought for the things of itself.

MONDAY—JANUARY 3.

MY grandmother had a scrapbook in which she used to jot down sayings and verses which had helped her. One of these I remember:

If any little word of mine can make a heart
the lighter,
If any little song of mine can make a life
the brighter,
Then let me speak my little word, and take my
bit of singing
And drop it in some lonely vale and set the
echoes ringing.

THE FRIENDSHIP BOOK

U THANT, a Buddhist, was for many years Secretary-General of the United Nations. He spent the first quarter of an hour or so of his day sitting quietly and meditating.

Once he was asked just what the nature of these meditations were and he replied, " I think of what is good in life—good thoughts, good deeds. It is difficult to explain exactly, but it is something like making a New Year resolution every day!"

Perhaps one of the problems about New Year resolutions is that they *are* made only once a year. Most of us need a more regular stimulus than that. How better to start the day than with thoughts of goodness so that these become part of the pattern of life and we can say hopefully of every morning, " This is the day which the Lord has made."

THE Lady of the House and I attended a New Year concert in the church hall. It was an informal affair with various members of our congregation taking part.

A special cheer went up as a rugged, 80-year old retired farmer rose to his feet.

" Just a wee recitation," he said, beaming at the audience. And this was it:

For every hill I've had to climb,
  For every stone that bruised my feet,
For all the blood and sweat and grime,
  For blinding storms and burning heat,
My heart sings but a grateful song—
These were the things that made me strong!

A wonderful way to look back on life, isn't it?

THURSDAY—JANUARY 6.

YEARS ago, after a visit to England, the eminent Polish scientist, Leopold Infeld, was asked what he liked best about it. He replied, " The knowledge that if I am walking along an English street and step on somebody's foot, I shall hear a very apologetic, ' I am so sorry '!"

I would like to think that manners have not deteriorated in the intervening years. It certainly increases our own happiness and lessens the embarrassment of others, thus warming human relationships, when people are not quick to think that it is always " the other person's fault."

FRIDAY—JANUARY 7.

I LIKE the thought behind these few lines:
Don't look for the flaws
As you go through life,
And even if you find 'em,
'Tis wise and kind to be somewhat blind,
And look for the virtues behind 'em.

SATURDAY—JANUARY 8.

HENRY FORD is credited with many sayings, perhaps the best known being: " You can have any colour of car you like so long as it's black."

Have you heard what his answer was when he was asked the question: " What is the difference between a wise man and a fool?"

He said: " Well, the wise man knows a thing can't be done and he doesn't find out that it can be done until some fool who doesn't know that it can't be done comes along and tries it and does it!"

MAJESTY

Nature's small miracles delight our gaze,
A dainty butterfly, a slender flower,
Yet there are places where, in sheer amaze,
We stand in awe of all her mighty power.

THE FRIENDSHIP BOOK

SUNDAY—JANUARY 9.

BE ye stedfast, unmoveable, always abounding in the work of the Lord, forasmuch as ye know that your labour is not in vain in the Lord.

MONDAY—JANUARY 10.

IN the days when candles were the common means of illumination there was an old saying, " Set your candle before the looking glass and you will have the light of two!"

I am not sure whether that is absolutely scientifically accurate, but there is sufficient truth in it to give us food for thought. I have a friend who always sets her vases of flowers in front of a mirror in a similar way and that certainly increases their beauty.

We are fond enough of magnifying our difficulties, of doubling our troubles. What a difference it would make to us and to those about us if we would start doing it with our blessings for a change. Let's see *them* double, too!

TUESDAY—JANUARY 11.

WHEN little Joanna was about six years old she had already learned to pray. One evening, before going to sleep, she knelt at her bedside and prayed: " Thank you, Jesus, for all the nice things I've eaten today. Thank you for the games I played. Thank you for the lovely flowers in the garden."

Her eyes flickered open for a moment, then closed again as she added: " And thank you, Jesus, that there is such a lot to thank you for. Amen."

Isn't it a beautiful prayer?

THE FRIENDSHIP BOOK

O NE of the greatest pleasures of life is conversation," wrote Sydney Smith, the early 19th-century clergyman, wit and writer. He himself was reckoned to be one of the greatest and most amusing conversationalists of his day.

Another was Dr Samuel Johnson who admired John Wesley's conversation though he complained that Wesley " was never at leisure, but always obliged to leave at a certain hour. This is very disagreeable to a man who loves to fold his legs and have his talk out as I do."

Have we friends? Have we leisure sometimes for quiet, pleasant conversation? Then we have treasure indeed!

W HEN I was a boy an old elm tree grew at the foot of our garden. Because it leaned heavily it was considered dangerous and had to be cut down. In falling, the elm uprooted and damaged a young sycamore growing on adjacent waste ground.

After the tree-fellers had removed the elm, I climbed over the fence to survey the damage. There lay the little twisted sycamore, its slender trunk fractured. I bound it up with adhesive tape and re-planted it.

Today that sycamore is a strong, healthy tree, standing straight and tall. The lower trunk is still distorted but the tree itself has risen proudly above the defect.

Whenever I see that tree it reminds me not to brood over past mistakes or imagined wrongs. It's today and tomorrow that count.

RIDING OUT

Goodbye to streets,
To city faces!
Hello, morning,
And lonely places . . .

THE FRIENDSHIP BOOK

A FRIEND I know walked by today,
  It made me feel downcast;
But when he turned and came to me,
  The time sped by so fast.
His joy and sparkle cheered me up,
  With such friends we can't fail.
As he left to go, I waved my hand,
  But he just wagged his tail!

POOR health forced our organist to retire at 70 years of age. For several Sundays he missed the services altogether so I called to see how he fared. I found him propped up in bed, his wheezy chest making conversation difficult.

While we sat in companionable silence I gazed round his room until a text arrested my attention. Or was it a text?

" And it came to pass," I read aloud. " That's an odd text, Andrew."

" Aye, but it's my favourite for all that," he whispered. " I'm glad the Bible doesn't say ' And it came to stay '."

I smiled as enlightenment dawned. Andrew had learned to take the rough with the smooth in life and was quietly confident that his illness, like all else, would one day be a thing of the past.

I had called to cheer my old friend up, but came away uplifted by his favourite text.

FOR I the lord thy God will hold thy right hand, saying unto thee, Fear not; I will help thee.

MONDAY—JANUARY 17.

A YORKSHIRE woman once sent her son to the local music teacher to take some piano lessons. After one or two futile attempts, the baffled instructor sent him back with the following note: " I can do nothing for your son—he has no ear for music."

" What does he mean?" snorted the outraged mother. " How dare he say such a thing? Our Billy's got a lug as big as a dinner plate!"

TUESDAY—JANUARY 18.

O NE thing nearly all older folk like to do is keep things that have long outlived their usefulness. And why not? They are mementoes of their more active days and therefore very dear to them. Mrs A. M. Fenn, who lives in an eventide home, sent me this verse on the subject. She calls it " Treasures."

In our Old People's Home
  There are treasures galore,
Beloved by their owners
  Who keep them in store.
Old letters written
  By writers now dead,
Books cherished in childhood,
  Though now seldom read.
Bits of cracked china
  More precious than gold,
Photos depicting
  The young grown old.
A useless collection
  Of rubbish you say—
But we haven't the heart
  Just to throw them away!

THE FRIENDSHIP BOOK

MOST of us have probably heard of the "Breeches Bible" and the "Vinegar Bible", but I wonder if we know about the "One Finger Bible"?

The story is that a 19th-century Russian Jew, Samuel Schereschewsky, went to America and was converted to Christianity.

A distinguished linguist, he visited China and decided to translate the Old Testament into Wenli Chinese. He had hardly started the task, however, when he was struck with paralysis and could not hold a pen between his fingers. Not to be defeated, he typed out the whole of his translation using only his middle finger.

When we become discouraged because of some disability it can often help to recall a story of courage and determination like this.

I READ somewhere of a man who made a collection of boxes of various kinds—trinket boxes, money boxes, glove boxes, cigar boxes and so on. Probably the most curious was a Japanese smiling box! It was beautifully decorated, but when you opened it and looked inside there was just a mirror in which you saw your own reflection—a surprise which apparently always makes the person looking inside smile.

If we all possessed a smiling box into which we could look when we felt sad, irritable or frustrated, the world might be a happier place and we should certainly be happier people. Perhaps it is almost worth making one—or at least imagining we have one and going through the motions!

SURPRISE

When things seem dull, don't despair!
Any moment, anywhere,
Round a corner you may chance
On excitement and romance.

THE FRIENDSHIP BOOK

THE young minister had embarked on a series of " special sermons " on topics which he had hoped might evoke some response from his congregation, but as the series drew to an end, he confided to an elderly member that nobody had said a word to him about the sermons.

" Ah, weel," was the reply, " if naebody has said aught agin 'em, they'll be all reet!"

That was probably true, but what a pity that often we speak only to criticise! A word of encouragement and appreciation can mean so much. " Thy words have set men on their feet," says a Biblical writer.

THE milkman called for his money this morning.
A dreary morning, and the milk had gone up in price yet again this week! However, our milkman is a cheery fellow, and often his whistle is the first thing I hear in the morning, so it would have been churlish to greet him with grumbles.

I was so glad I restrained myself—he swung up the garden path. " 'Morning," he carolled cheerfully—" January almost over, soon be April, brighter sun, warmer days, bulbs blooming, birds singing—keep smiling!"

My goodness, how much brighter the day seemed after that—I didn't even begrudge the rise in the price any more.

THE fear of the Lord is the beginning of wisdom.

IT is said that, after many years of service with a famous duke, a cook gave in his notice. His friends were surprised that he should give up so good and secure a job, but when asked about it he said, " If I serve up a good dinner I never get a word of praise from the Duke. If the meal goes wrong in some way he never speaks a word of blame. So what is the use of working for him?"

Most people will accept blame where they know it is due, but they do like a word of praise too when that is due. It it not a matter of pride—it is simply that to know that what one does is appreciated brings a glow of well-being. We can spread a lot of happiness if we look for opportunities to speak a word of encouragement and appreciation.

WHEN Dr Herbert Lockyer, the well-known religious author and preacher, reached the age of 80, he told of an old lady of similar age who used to say, proudly, " I am now an octogeranium."

Bless her heart!" was Dr Lockyer's comment. " Doubtless she had learned to grow old beautifully!"

Certainly the good doctor himself had learned the art of growing old gracefully and continued through his writings to bring inspiration to ordinary people.

His secret perhaps lay in a verse he often quoted:

You will never grow old if you have a goal
And a purpose to achieve,
You will never grow old if you have the power
To dream and to believe.

THE FRIENDSHIP BOOK

WEDNESDAY—JANUARY 26.

LAURIE LEE, the poet and novelist, shares the all too common handicap of a degree of deafness, but he does not let it get him down. In an interview he shrugged it off by saying, " The things you think you hear are often more interesting than what is actually being said!" He told how he once hurried across a London street to see if he could help someone who was apparently calling out in distress, " Oh! I can't stand it!" only to find that it was a newspaper seller calling, " Star, News and Standard!"

Of course, deafness can be embarrassing and frustrating, but, as with all life's handicaps, seeing the lighter side of the situation can greatly ease the burden. If we have a sense of humour, and an ability to look on the brighter side, we may truly thank God for two of His good gifts.

THURSDAY—JANUARY 27.

THE day after the Great War broke out in 1914, Sir Edward Grey (later, Viscount Grey), the Foreign Secretary, wrote to a musician whose singing had greatly delighted him at a concert he had attended. In his letter he said: " I love Handel's music, and it does me good. Europe is in the most terrible trouble it has ever known in civilised times and no one can say what will be left at the end. But Handel's music will survive."

That someone caught up in the very heart of turmoil as Edward Grey was, should find solace in music, is a reminder to us of the power of music to speak to our hearts and renew our spirits. We need not be great musicians to appreciate its influence. All we have to do is listen . . .

FRIDAY—JANUARY 28.

IN her book, *The Joy of Children*, Pearl Buck wrote, " If I were asked what element is most important in a child's life, I would say the element of beauty . . . they must be taught to discover beauty in Nature, in art, in music and books, in noble human beings living or dead, in the loyalties of friendship and family, in the love of country and of God."

But how true this is for all of us—not just for children. Ugliness is all too easy to find; we need to search out beauty so that faith and love may be restored. Remember what Tertullian, the second century theologian said: " If I give you a rose you won't doubt God any more."

SATURDAY—JANUARY 29.

WHO was the finest orator who ever lived? We can never settle that argument, but the speeches of Demosthenes, a Greek who lived 2400 years ago, are still quoted by speakers as supreme examples of their art.

Demosthenes had a stammer and a weak voice—not much of a start for a man who desperately wanted to become the greatest speaker of his day.

To cure his stammer he spoke with pebbles in his mouth. To strengthen his voice he recited poems as he ran up-hill. To get used to the sound of a crowd he made speeches standing by the sea-shore. And to perfect the art of speech-writing he worked for months in a cave underground.

Men and women don't change. If we want badly enough to do something we will find a way—as Demosthenes did 24 centuries ago.

THE FRIENDSHIP BOOK

THOU hast delivered my soul from death, mine eyes from tears, and my feet from falling.

OVER 150 years ago Robert Collyer was one of the small boys awakened and summoned to work by the harsh clang of the factory bell in the village of Fewston in Yorkshire. Robert emigrated and eventually became Minister of the Church of the Messiah in New York. He was a preacher, scholar and poet of distinction, and he often spoke of the melancholy sound of the bell.

When he heard that the old factory was being demolished he wrote to a friend and said that if the bell was being broken up he would like a piece to remind him of his early days. To his consternation, the whole bell arrived!

At first he did not know what to do with it—then he remembered that one of the departments of Cornell University had no bell so he offered it to the authorities warning them that it "made the worst clangour that ever vexed the heavens". They accepted the gift and invited Robert Collyer to ring it for the first time.

He pulled the rope, hardening himself against the anticipated din. To his astonishment the sound of the bell rang out sweet and clear across the campus! He realised that the harsh sound he remembered must have been only in the imagination of a sleepy, overworked little boy and not in the bell at all.

It's worth reminding ourselves that sometimes we blame our circumstances for what is in ourselves.

FEBRUARY

TUESDAY—FEBRUARY 1.

O N cold, wet mornings the Lady of the House sometimes invites our postman in for a cup of tea to warm him up on his round. I know he appreciates it, though, if truth be told, he is always cheerful and smiling even without our hospitality, and his smile and happy greeting have brightened many a dull day for us.

One particularly bad morning when he had been trudging through the deep snow, I said to him, " The weather never seems able to get you down." " Well," was his reply, " I treat each day as my own, and a sunny day as a very special personal gift!"

No wonder he can smile, come wind, come rain!

WEDNESDAY—FEBRUARY 2.

I N Lockhart's *Life of Sir Walter Scott* we are told that in the grounds of his home at Abbotsford there was a summerhouse which was often used by Peter Mathieson, Scott's coachman, as a quiet place for his devotions. Scott would sometimes linger for a few moments within hearing distance, gaining spiritual refreshment and inspiration from the old man's prayers.

Old Peter would probably have been amazed if he had known that the great author derived new strength from listening to what he said to God, but don't you find it an appealing picture—the famous writer standing in the garden, listening humbly to the simple prayers of an old servant?

THE FRIENDSHIP BOOK

OVER the years I have heard a great number of supposed " cures " for worry, but one of the most ingenious and I suspect one of the most effective was that of a man who advocated worrying for 10 minutes a day!

His technique was to jot down over a period of time everything that worried him. Then, when he had collected several sheets of worries, he set apart a period each day for worrying . . . brooding on the things he had written down.

After five or ten minutes of doing this he found the procedure so ludicrous that he began to get worry into perspective until he stopped bothering altogether. It's worth trying. You may well find two minutes quite long enough to convince you that you're wasting your time!

YOU know what a chameleon is, don't you, Mr Gay?"

Young Billy often asks me questions if I'm in the garden when he's coming home from school.

" I think so," I said. " It's a lizard that can change colour to suit its surroundings."

" Right," said Billy. " If I put a chameleon on a brown carpet it would change colour—to what?"

" To brown, I suppose!" I answered.

" Quite right, Mr Gay. And on a red carpet?"

" It would go red, wouldn't it?"

" Now, Mr Gay, here's the really difficult question. What colour would it go if you put it on a tartan kilt?"

" You young rascal . . ." I called out. But he was up the road like a flash!

UNFORGETTABLE

A happy day flies past too soon
As hours and minutes measure,
But memory stores a lasting boon
Of recollected pleasure.

THE FRIENDSHIP BOOK

THE Rev. Harold S. Hulbert, children's evangelist and Methodist minister, once made this accurate and telling observation: " Children need love, especially when they don't deserve it."

None of us, if we are honest, *deserve* love. But how much we all *need* it!

THE Lord is my rock, and my fortress, and my deliverer.

MOST of the gardeners I know seem to have a bit of the philosopher about them, and this was confirmed by something a friend told me recently. During some gardening classes he was attending, he acquired three amaryllis bulbs. He gave them all exactly the same treatment, but while two of them bore magnificent flowers the third produced nothing but a mass of long, green leaves.

Puzzled, he took it to his gardening tutor who examined it and prodded it and then said, " Well, for reasons best known to herself, Mother Nature has decided that it will not flower this year."

" Shall I throw it out, then?" Asked my friend.

" Oh, no!" was the reply. " It will probably flower next year." Then, with a twinkle in his eye, he added, " Just look after it and regard it as an aspidistra with promise!"

When we look at life's disappointments with hope and expectancy of better things, what a difference it makes! Remember, " The best is yet to be."

TUESDAY—FEBRUARY 8.

I EXPECT you know that grand old chorus, " Count your blessings . . ." Yet really our blessings are uncountable, aren't they? Just stop a moment and make a list of them: Sight, smell, hearing, a home, the next meal, good shoes . . . What, you don't count the ordinary everyday things as blessings? You consider maybe that we're entitled to them, and only the " big " things in life should be called blessings?

Um, well I call these extras our " bonus awards "!

WEDNESDAY—FEBRUARY 9.

SOME friends of ours really believe in " getting away from it all " when they go on holiday. They stay in a little country cottage lit by oil lamps and they have to walk several hundred yards to a spring for water.

" Makes you very careful with the water," they said, " when you have to carry it all." Then they told us a story of someone who had holidayed under similar conditions. " He washed the tea cups and saucers and, as the water still looked perfectly clean, he rinsed out the tea towel in it. Then he washed the dog, and then the floor, and finally, threw it out to water the garden!"

What a lot you can do with a little! David with his sling and stones. The lad with his five loaves and two fishes. Jesus and His twelve disciples. Multitudes of ordinary folk with quite ordinary gifts. Don't let's despise what sometimes seems to be the smallness of our resources. It is amazing what a lot can be accomplished with a little if only we are prepared to use our resources to the full.

THE FRIENDSHIP BOOK

I WAS very impressed with these lines titled " An Apology ". Most of us need to make one sometimes, and this is what I read:

An apology is a friendship preserver,
Is often a debt of honour,
Is never a sign of weakness,
Is an antidote for hatred,
Costs nothing but one's pride,
Always saves more than it costs,
Is needed in every home.

JOHN RUSKIN, the artist, writer and art critic, was a great admirer of the paintings of Turner and he had a number of them on the walls of his house, Brantwood, on the shores of Lake Coniston in Cumbria. However, these pictures were hung rather haphazardly, not arranged as neatly and attractively as some of his friends thought they ought to be to show them off to the best advantage.

One day a friend ventured to remark on this to Ruskin. He replied thoughtfully, " You know, that sort of thing doesn't bother me much. I don't look *at* pictures; I look *into* them."

I suspect that Ruskin saw far more than most people. How much more we should get out of life if we cultivated the art not just of looking casually *at* things, but of really looking *into* them! It doesn't apply only to pictures but to all our surroundings—indoor as well as outdoor—to the people we meet, the things we read, and all the rest. Try it, and see the difference it makes. You will find riches you never dreamed of.

IN one of his inspirational books, *Word Power—Life Power,* Vernon Howard tells of a man who had 15 steps leading to his garden. He walked up these many times in the course of a day, but instead of regarding the process as a bit of a toil he used his imagination to make them a means of self-development. In his mind he gave each step the name of a quality he wanted to cultivate or improve in himself—patience, optimism, determination and so on. As he ascended the steps, he imagined himself growing in these qualities. His progress up the steps was progress towards a fuller life.

It may sound a little juvenile, but it worked for him. There are other things we might try, too; there is so much about us that, used imaginatively, can become a source of inspiration—a quiet scene, to deepen our tranquillity; the laughter of children at play to give us happiness; the beauty of a garden to develop beauty of character. Imagination is a potent force—when we use it for good it can work wonders in us.

WHAT is man, that thou art mindful of him? And the son of man, that thou visitest him?

IT isn't often I come upon a proverb from Turkey, but I happened on this one the other day and knew at once I had to pass it on:

" The devil tempts the busy man—but the idle man tempts the devil."

THE FRIENDSHIP BOOK

ON Shrove Tuesday at Westminster School, a pancake is annually scrambled for, in what is known as the Pancake Greeze. At 11 o'clock the cook, preceded by the verger with a silver-topped mace, enters the great schoolroom, carrying a frying pan from which he tosses a pancake over the high bar separating the old Upper and Lower Schools. The boys scramble for the pancake as it falls to the ground and the one who seizes it, or the largest piece of it, receives a prize from the Dean.

All good fun, no doubt, but not much of a lesson for life. There are far too many people in the world scrambling to get the biggest and best of everything for themselves.

Better to remember the words of Sir Wilfred Grenfell: "No thinker can believe that the worthwhileness of life is what we get out of it. No one enters life, or school, or club, or country, or marriage, possessed of that spirit will find any human institution a success."

It is what we put in, not what we get out which makes life worth while.

WEDNESDAY—FEBRUARY 16.

I EXPECT you've heard of the wisdom of Socrates, but did you know he was quite a sociable fellow at heart? It is said that when he was having a new house built in Athens a passer-by stopped and asked him why the building was so small. " Surely a great man deserves a much grander house?" said the man.

The philosopher shook his head. " This house will be big enough," he said. " I will be happy in it as along as it is filled with real friends."

C

RICHARD JEFFERIES, the 19th century naturalist and writer, spent much of his life struggling against poverty and ill-health. Yet, confined to his invalid chair, he wrote: " Every blade of grass was mine as if I had planted it. All the grasses were my pets; I loved them all. Every wild hawk that passed overhead was mine. What more beautiful than the sweep and curve of his going through the azure sky? Oh, happy, happy days! So beautiful to watch—and all mine!"

What a difference it makes to our outlook when in this kind of way we can feel that the world—the whole world—is ours to enjoy.

IN her lifetime, Maureen, who lives on the beautiful Isle of Man, has had occasion to visit many different countries, and a short time ago she shared her thoughts on the so-called problem of race relations.

She found the ordinary folk so helpful all over the world. A villainous-looking Indian taxi driver in Bombay stopped without being asked and obtained a large piece of ice for her son's nose-bleed. A German shop assistant went to great trouble to find the right size of support tights—although Maureen couldn't speak German and the assistant knew no English. And a Japanese businessman sent a bottle of wine to their table to wish them a happy stay in his country—although they had never spoken to him before.

Isn't it true that ordinary folk, of every nationality, and every language, know the art of friendship?

SATURDAY—FEBRUARY 19.

DO you know what P.B.P.G.I.N.T.W.M.Y. stands for? I saw the letters on a young friend's badge the other evening.

When I asked I was told that they stand for "Please Be Patient. God Is Not Through With Me Yet". Not at all a bad motto for those of us aspiring to the best and yet aware of how much further we still have to go.

SUNDAY—FEBRUARY 20.

THE Lord also will be a refuge for the oppressed, a refuge in times of trouble.

MONDAY—FEBRUARY 21.

THE name of Dick Sheppard, radio preacher and Vicar of St. Martin-in-the-Fields, London, lives on in the memory of many over 40 years after his death. Many are the stories told of his understanding and compassion.

He once visited an army camp and, to the astonishment of the resident chaplain, was seen to be in happy conversation with a man whom everybody else regarded as difficult and unapproachable.

"However did you manage that, Dr. Sheppard?" asked the chaplain. "I haven't been able to get near that man in six months."

"Oh," was the reply, "I asked after his mother and told him two funny stories."

Perhaps we sometimes try too hard with "difficult" people. Dick Sheppard had that light touch, that simple concern which could help us all in our relationships with one another.

GRANPA had promised to take young David for a walk, so there they were, going up the hill behind the farm where they were on holiday. Only, after a few minutes Granpa was sure it was young David taking Granpa for a walk!

When they got to the top of the hill David took to his heels and raced down the other side, making the two of them look like the tortoise and the hare.

On the way back they had to climb a gate and here Granpa's longer legs gave him an advantage so that he was over first. He began to walk on.

" Hey, Granpa," shouted a young voice, " aren't you going to wait for me?"

" But you didn't wait for me," said Granpa, thinking he would give David a practical lesson in fair play.

" But you caught up, didn't you, Granpa, so it didn't really matter," replied David, as he held out his hands for a help over the gate.

Sometimes it's hard to win!

THE Lady of the House and I were walking round our local garden centre and as we paused by the greenhouses we saw a man carefully examining one while his wife looked patiently on. Then quietly she asked, " Do you think you will be able to get your bed into that one, Peter?"

She was smiling broadly, so she was not being bitter and he laughed, too, as he told the salesman, " I'll take it."

Where would a man be without his hobbies and where would wives be without their occasional grumbles!

FOUR young men were discussing the merits of various translations of the Bible. Three of them mentioned specific versions of the Bible, but the fourth was silent.

When pressed for his opinion, he replied, " I like my mother's translation best. She translated it into life, and it was the most convincing translation I ever saw."

THE late Dr. W.E. Sangster once wrote about what he called " minute prayers ". I never actually heard him *say* the word " minute " so I am not sure whether he meant it in the sense of " tiny ", or of prayers which could be said in 60 seconds. It amounts to the same thing, I suppose. Prayers do not need to be lengthy. Here are some little gems of prayer which we can use at any time, anywhere.

" O Lord, let me not live to be useless."
(John Wesley)

" Protect me, my Lord, my boat is so small, and your ocean so big."
(Breton fishermen's prayer)

" Lead kindly Light, amid the encircling gloom, Lead Thou me on."
(J.H. Newman)

" Grant, O Lord, that I may be like a fire that illumines and warms, like a fountain that takes away thirst, like a tree that shelters and protects."
(Hindu prayer)

" O God help me to be master of myself that I may be a servant of others."
(Source unknown)

MIRACLE

The weather forecast's gloomy,
  More blizzards still in store,
When suddenly you notice,
  Though winter winds still roar,
A miracle in the garden —
  It's snowdrop time once more!

K INDNESS is a language the dumb can speak, and the deaf hear and understand."

We don't know who coined that description, but I think it's lovely. Don't you?

W E will rejoice in thy salvation, and in the name of our God we will set up our banners.

I T was a sad day for Christine Olivier of Christchurch when her four-year-old daughter died of an obscure illness.

But she refused to brood upon it. And with the kind of courage which only those who have experienced that kind of bereavement can fully appreciate, she began to exercise a ministry to others.

Each day she would scan the newspaper columns, and every time she saw the announcement of a child's death, she would write to the bereaved parents and express her sympathy, saying how well she understood, because she, too, had lost a little one.

In her letter she would refer the parents to the One who could give comfort and consolation, and invite them to her church, if they did not already have a church allegiance, for she knew her minister would be glad to help in any way he could.

Many otherwise distraught parents have blessed Christine Olivier for her ministry of love and sympathy. And isn't it true that a sorrow shared is a sorrow at least halved?

MARCH

TUESDAY—MARCH 1.

I MAKE no comment on these challenging words that were once spoken by King George V:

"The foundations of national glory are set in the homes of the people, and they will only remain unshaken while the family life of our race is strong, simple, and pure."

WEDNESDAY—MARCH 2.

HAVE you noticed how poignantly certain smells can recall a childhood memory? I passed a bakery and the delicious aroma of freshly baked bread reminded me of plump-faced Mrs Dingle—"Auntie Ding-dong" we children called her. She used to bake bread and take it to needy families and she had a smile for all as she carried her basket covered with a spotless napkin.

Once when my mother was in bed with flu Auntie Ding-dong brought us a large loaf still warm from her oven and how the smell made my mouth water!

She had been left a widow while she was still quite young and could have spent a miserable life wallowing in self-pity. Instead she spent her days helping others.

"Me ever feel sorry for myself?" she once exclaimed to a neighbour. "Why, I haven't the time!"

As I passed the bakery the other day I was grateful for the recollection of a lovely person who had her own recipe for happiness as well as for delicious bread.

THE FRIENDSHIP BOOK

OVER the fireplace of The Eagles, Penmachno, a public house in North Wales, is this encouraging inscription which I am sure we would do well to take to heart:

Fear knocked at the door;
Faith answered it;
Nobody was there.

I SAT fascinated by an illustrated lecture on the Natural History of New Zealand. The lecturer had much to tell us, and told it with great enthusiasm. Amongst his many stories was that of a colony of strange lizard-like animals called tuataras that live on a small rocky island just off the mainland.

I say "strange" because they are the only three-eyed creatures in the world. Yet, according to scientists, they long ago stopped using the third eye. A few generations more and the third eye will be lost for ever.

He also told us about the kiwi, a flightless bird and therefore constantly in danger from predators. The kiwi, he explained, wasn't always flightless. At one time it had a pair of fine wings, but it didn't use them, and so as generation followed generation, the wings became less and less useful, until all it has now is a little pair of flappers, useless for flight.

"What we don't use, we lose," he finished.

I felt I had heard these stories, or one like them, before and then I remembered where—in the parable of the talents. Read it again today and you will see what I mean.

SATURDAY—MARCH 5.

PETER MARSHALL, the much-loved Scottish-born Chaplain to the United States Senate, once prayed: " Lord, when we are wrong, make us willing to change, and when we are right, make us easy to live with."

SUNDAY—MARCH 6.

LIFT up your hearts, O ye gates; and be ye lift up, ye everlasting doors; and the King of glory shall come in.

MONDAY—MARCH 7.

THERE is a story told of H. H. Asquith after he had been defeated as Member of Parliament for Paisley in 1924. He had served the constituency for 38 years in this position and the blow was unexpected. His daughter, Lady Violet Bonham-Carter, said of the event: " As we steamed out of the station I lay back in the carriage feeling bruised from head to foot. I looked across at my father in an agony of solicitude and suddenly realised by his calm gaze, that he had already made peace with events."

It is sometimes not disasters themselves that defeat people, but the fretting and fuming resulting from them. That is where " acceptance " or " making peace with events " can be such a help. One has only to notice the difference between two people struck down with the same sort of illness. One cries and rages in turn; the other smiles and accepts the situation, reflecting that things could have been worse and there is hope for improvement.

THE FRIENDSHIP BOOK

AN Englishman was trying to persuade a Chinaman to enter a house which was guarded by a barking dog.

"Come on," he said. "You know the proverb, 'A barking dog never bites'?"

"Yes," said the Chinaman doubtfully, "*I* know proverb; *you* know proverb; but does *the dog* know proverb?"

FOR 90 years the great railway bridge across the Forth in Scotland has been one of the engineering wonders of the world, made familiar on millions of "snaps" and picture postcards.

But there was a moment when William Arrol, who built it, must have wondered if it was all going to tumble into the waters below.

The vast steel towers had been built, but still lacking were the arms which would link the towers and make the whole structure rigid, able to resist any wind that might come. The bridge was vulnerable.

At this critical stage a gale blew up the river. William Arrol stood, a solitary figure on a hillside, watching the wind pounding at his life's dream.

For a long time he stood watching. Then he turned and strode away. "It will stand," he said firmly.

It has—for almost a century.

You and I will never build a Forth Bridge but we can all be in a position where something we have said or done has to stand on its own and nothing we can do can alter the course of events.

It is then we know just how well we have built.

THURSDAY—MARCH 10.

ON my way home the other evening I heard two boys shouting at each other. As I drew near they fell to the ground fighting, arms and legs flaying.

"Is it worth it?" I asked. Somehow the question just slipped out as I looked down at them. The result was instantaneous. The two lads got up, grinned at one another and then ran off together. No one could have been more astonished than I!

I don't say that question will work every time, but if you know a couple who have had a quarrel and haven't yet made it up, why not try it? You might even find it a good question to put to yourself some time. I don't promise you it will work, but, remembering those two boys, I think there's a pretty good chance!

FRIDAY—MARCH 11.

WANDERING round a museum of domestic "by-gones" recently the Lady of the House and I came across a lace-maker's lamp and globe—something we had heard of, but never seen before. The globe was filled with water and the tiny lamp placed behind it. The small light was thus concentrated and magnified and the lace-maker could direct a disc of bright light exactly on the spot needed where the delicate and intricate work was being done.

I couldn't help thinking of the verse of a hymn:
The daily round, the trivial task
Will furnish all we ought to ask.

The humblest work can be done, " in a pool of light " so to speak, when we bring to it enthusiasm and a sense of the value of work.

SATURDAY—MARCH 12.

MARTIN LUTHER, in his autobiography, tells of one preacher he loved better than any other. He was, he said, " My tame little robin, who preaches to me daily. I put his crumbs upon my window-sill, especially at night. He hops on to the window-sill when he wants his supply, and takes as much as he desires to satisfy his need. From thence he always hops to a little tree close by and lifts up his voice to God and sings his carols of praise and gratitude, tucks his little head under his wing and goes fast to sleep, and leaves tomorrow to look after itself.

" He is the best preacher that I have on earth."

SUNDAY—MARCH 13.

THE law of the Lord is perfect, converting the soul: the testimony of the Lord is sure, making wise the simple.

MONDAY—MARCH 14.

AFTER Lotte Lehmann retired from opera singing many years ago a young soprano said to her, " It must be terrible for a great singer like you to realise that you have lost your voice."

" Not at all," was the reply. " What would be terrible would be if I didn't realise it!"

In the Greek temple of Delphi were written the words of an anonymous Greek writer, " Know thyself." To know our own strengths and weaknesses is perhaps one of the hardest bits of knowledge to acquire, but it is certainly one of the most worthwhile. In it lies a good deal of our own happiness—and that of all those around us.

IN OUR POWER

*A lump of clay the potter takes
And from it things of beauty makes.
So you and I, if we incline,
Can mould our lives to something fine.*

THE FRIENDSHIP BOOK

A WELL-KNOWN Baptist minister, the late Rev. F. Townley Lord, used to tell a story of an old violinist who was not a brilliant musician but simply had a great love of music. From his battered old violin he could coax music which never failed to charm the hearer. Asked to explain his secret he would hold out his violin and, tenderly caressing its curves, would say, " A great deal of sunshine must have gone into this wood, and what has gone in comes out."

Whether that is true of violins or not it is certainly true of lives. If our hearts and minds are open to the goodness and gladness all about us then, without our knowing it, happiness will radiate from us.

I HAVE an old country friend, well into his 80's now, who readily admits he never had any education worth mentioning. The habit of hard physical work was ground into him as a young boy, he grew up in that habit and it has stayed with him all his long life.

" I'm just an ignorant old fellow," he says. " I know nothing of sculpture or poetry, foreign languages or science and all such things."

And yet he knows the intricate habits of bees, the haunts of birds and other wild creatures, the sculpture of the landscape, the poetry of trees. He can read the clouds and winds more accurately than any scientific weather man. His very soul has captured the music and language of the earth.

No, my friend is certainly not ignorant, very far from it.

THURSDAY—MARCH 17.

IN preparation for a coming event, little Joan had been told that Daddy was ordering a small brother.

Triplets arrived, and when Joan heard this, she said to her mother, " Oh, dear, you should have ordered the baby yourself—you know how Daddy stutters!"

FRIDAY—MARCH 18.

I HAVE never felt more inspired by a book than I was when I had finished Pat Seed's *One Day At A Time*.

Pat had been told she had cancer and there seemed no chance of recovery. When in the depths of despair she saw a goal—to raise £1 million to buy a CAT Scanner for a Manchester hospital. This is a wonderful machine that can diagnose cancer early enough to make the difference between life and death.

An impossible aim for a woman with no private means and no special influence? Well, like the title of her book, one day at a time, with a multitude of well-wishers she reached her impossible goal. Yet all through her book she emphasises that she is a very ordinary woman.

Perhaps there is a little bit of Pat Seed in every man and woman. To have a goal can make a person do extraordinary things. And if, after all, we do fail? I don't know who wrote these words but they sum up what I feel:

One broken dream is not the end of dreaming,
One shattered hope is not the end of all;
Beyond the storm and tempest, stars are gleaming,
Still build your castles, though your castles fall.

THE FRIENDSHIP BOOK

I SUPPOSE it sounds strange if I say I feel sorry for our old apple tree in winter. But it's true. It has such a sad, empty look about it. In fact, when the season is bleakest I sometimes wonder whether the poor tree has died.

But then I am proved wrong. At the first hint of spring the tree is reborn. The branches are suddenly arrayed in a shimmering haze of delicate green lace. Tight little buds burst forth into glorious blossom. Once again the miracle of spring shows me a lesson for living.

All the while I thought the tree was dead it was only outwardly dormant. Hidden inside, new life was being nurtured ready to make its debut at just the right time.

Things may look forlorn, even hopeless at times. But have faith—a wonderful change is coming.

SUNDAY—MARCH 20.

HE maketh me to lie down in green pastures: he leadeth me beside the still waters.

MONDAY—MARCH 21.

GOD must have loved us, I say, when I see
Spring bursting out in each flower and tree.
The song of the blackbird who's courting his mate,
The sweet scent of primroses down by the gate,
The sun on my back getting warmer each day,
The promise of blossom on hedges of may:
Though I know in this world there is much that's amiss
I know He must love us to give us all this.

D

TUESDAY—MARCH 22.

A SIX-YEAR-OLD boy was needing a kidney transplant. One kidney had already been removed, and the remaining organ was not functioning. The only possible donor was the boy's twin brother.

His brother at once said that he was going to give his brother his right kidney, and when asked why, the lad replied: " Because I'm right-handed, so my right kidney must be the strongest, and I want to give my brother the best one."

Love demands our best, doesn't it?

WEDNESDAY—MARCH 23.

MY wife and I have a friend who is rather possessive. We like him a great deal, but he does tend to swamp us with his affections. You could call him a pushy fellow, though I think he'd die for us, if need be.

If we should ever be so unkind as to leave him out of things he does not complain. He just sits and sulks. When we include him in he lavishes so much love on us that we feel uncomfortable.

He follows us like a slave all day and he guards us by night. When out walking he is good company; he never argues. When I'm glad, he's glad. When I'm sad, he's sad. In fact, the more I think about it the more I realise his worth. Because there are times when he sits quietly at my feet and gives a certain look—as though he's trying to help me solve my petty problems. And that is when I reach out and hug my four-footed friend.

There's nothing quite like the adoring gaze of large, soppy, brown eyes when you need to get things in perspective.

THE FRIENDSHIP BOOK

SHEILA O'DONNELL was a district midwife in Dublin. One night she was called out quite late, and with a woman doctor as her companion, made her way through several dark lanes and alleyways until Sheila was quite certain they were hopelessly lost.

However, she stole a glance at the doctor when they passed the next lamp, and was reassured by the unperturbed look on her face. Minutes later they reached the house in question, delivered the baby, and then both returned to St Columba's Hospital.

It was only then that the doctor confessed that on the way to the patient's house *she* had been feeling terrified, but that Sheila had looked so calm that she had given her courage!

I READ somewhere that the Chinese primrose, sometimes seen in greenhouses here, will bear red flowers if it is grown at a temperature of about 60 degrees. If it is grown at a higher temperature, however, the colour of the flowers will change from red to white. We can turn up the temperature and change the appearance of the flower.

In all sorts of ways too we can alter the "temperature" and "atmosphere" of our surroundings in a way that changes people as well. A little more warmth of friendship, of sympathy, of encouragement on our part and what a difference it can make to those with whom we come in contact, who may be feeling lonely, depressed or discouraged. Let's turn up the temperature and look for the changes it can make!

THE FRIENDSHIP BOOK

I *T is hard to say you're sorry,*
  Admit you're in the wrong.
But eating humble pie can make
  The weakest will grow strong.
And, in the owning-up, there'll be
Your self-respect restored—you'll see.

SUNDAY—MARCH 27.

THE words of the Lord are pure words: as silver tried in a furnace of earth, purified seven times.

MONDAY—MARCH 28.

GEORGE, the factory nightwatchman, was on duty on the night in March when clocks had to be put forward one hour at the beginning of British Summer Time. His extra duties that night involved altering the scores of clocks in the factory.

On weekends he used to go straight home to bed when his stint was over, but on Sundays he had his breakfast at the factory and then went on to church before going home.

On this particular morning, as he arrived at church he found to his astonishment that the congregation was coming away! Then he remembered. He had altered all the clocks in the factory, but had forgotten to alter his own!

If we are honest with ourselves we know that often we are better at putting other people right than at putting ourselves right. This was surely the point of the parable Jesus told about the man trying to pluck a splinter out of his neighbour's eye when he had a plank sticking out of his own!

THE FRIENDSHIP BOOK

THE editor of a city paper was so annoyed at certain happenings in municipal affairs that he headlined his article on the subject: " Half The City Council Are Crooks ".

Not surprisingly, several councillors objected to this headline and demanded that the editor publish an apology or a suitably amended headline. The revised headline duly appeared: " Half The City Council Are Not Crooks ".

THE easiest thing in the world is finding fault. And have you noticed that the people who find fault oftenest are seldom happy people?

I'm sure Joyce Grenfell knew this well. Shortly after this much-loved woman had died I listened to tributes being paid to her memory. Nothing so much impressed me as a simple statement from an actress who had worked beside her in the theatre:

" Joyce looked for good in everybody and because she looked she found it."

SHE is the type of person in whom laughter bubbles up like a natural spring. Her smile brings light just when you've hit a dark patch. Her arm around your shoulder offers strength even before you need it. When you are feeling low she talks kindly, and before long she has you chuckling over some past remembered incident.

Have you got a friend like that? If so, treasure her. She is the sunshine of your life and a source of real joy.

EVER NEW

It's never dull to live beside a river
Sharing its moods that alter day by day,
So that each dweller keeps in touch with Nature
And learns the secrets of the water's way.

APRIL

FRIDAY—APRIL 1.

I LOVE to watch a christening. Some folk, I know, say what's the use of sprinkling drops of water on the head of a baby who doesn't know what is happening. But to me there is something moving beyond words in a baby being received into a community which promises to love it and cherish it.

These thoughts came to me with new force after a friend had told me of an experience in the ancient little church of Linton in the Scottish Borders.

He had driven along country roads in the April sunshine and climbed the path to the top of the mound on which the church stands. There was to be a double christening—something that had not happened at Linton for many, many years.

The babies were as good as gold until near the end of the ceremony, when one became restless. The minister, the Rev. Joe Brown, paused in what he was saying, leant over the pulpit and, with the knowledge of a man who has seen many christenings, suggested, " Try her on the other arm, Mary."

Mary did, and it worked like a charm.

" I'll never forget that day," said my friend. " The little old church, the sun shining, the birds singing outside and two babies being received into the church and into the community, as had been happening there, generation after generation."

It's a privilege to be present on such an occasion, yet the wonderful thing is it's a privilege open to us all.

THE FRIENDSHIP BOOK

THE barrow boy was doing brisk trade with his tomatoes. Then one woman, having counted her change, turned back and said: " I think you've given me ten pence too much in my change." The man counted the change in her hand and agreed. The woman gave him the ten pence, and was about to move away again, when he called her back. " Just a minute, luv," he said. " Let me look in that bag a sec." He opened it, and removed a squashy, unprepossessing tomato, and put a good sound one back in its place. " All square," he grinned, albeit a bit sheepishly.

HE is not here: for he is risen, as he said. Come, see the place where the Lord lay.

THE LOVELIEST THING

THE loveliest thing I have seen today?
It was not the lambs on the hillside fair,
Nor the sails that danced on the sunlit bay,
Or the bird that skimmed through the warm clear
air.
It was not the flowers that blossomed sweet,
Or the clover I crushed beneath my feet,
Or the strong wide spread of the old oak tree.
Not one of these things, or any other,
But the way that a little one turned from me
And the look that he gave to his fond young
mother.
The most beautiful thing I have seen today
Was the look in that youngster's eyes, I'd say!

THE FRIENDSHIP BOOK

HOW beautiful the spring flowers are; beautiful in form, in colour, and beautiful in promise. Gone are the dull, dark winters, and we can now look ahead to longer, brighter days, with trees and flowers in full glory.

Now it is Easter-time, and in my garden a clump of modest, frail little lily-of-the-valley is coming into bloom. To me this clump is always a miracle, because it appears where some previous owner of the garden had decided that a concrete path should be, and so within this tomb the lilies-of-the-valley were sealed. But come Easter-time and a wonderful thing happens—through the tiny cracks appear the stems, rising up stronger and stronger, with each delicate bell as it opens seeming to ring a peal of victory—" See, I have overcome death, I have risen from the tomb!"

WEDNESDAY—APRIL 6.

ELSIE had been going through a hard time fighting depression. At one point she felt overwhelmed with despair. She thought the whole world was against her. Then, one day, tired and dispirited, she returned home to find on the kitchen table a freshly-baked Dundee cake her neighbour had made specially for her.

" I made a pot of tea, then cut a slice of the cake," she told me later, " and while I was eating it I suddenly felt happy. The depression lifted and I felt new hope—all because my neighbour had shown that she cared."

Elsie is feeling much better now and she says her recovery is not so much due to her doctor as to her neighbour and that Dundee cake!

THURSDAY—APRIL 7.

I CAME home the other evening to find the Lady of the House chuckling over one of the day's happenings. Soon I was chuckling, too. She had gone to call on a young mother down the road. Little David had been in the garden and he had watched her try to open the gate. At last it had opened and she walked up the path.

"I could have told you how to open it," said David very seriously, "but I didn't because it's supposed to keep me in."

FRIDAY—APRIL 8.

HIS name may have been Job. He was an elderly man, and had endured many of the ills of life in his 77 years. His friends had great sympathy for him, and once suggested that he had borne more troubles than anyone else.

His reply showed the spirit of true wisdom and true peace: "Yes, my friends, that is true. I have been surrounded by troubles all my life long. But the curious thing about them is that nine-tenths of them never happened to me."

SATURDAY—APRIL 9.

ACCORDING to a leading medical authority, talking to pets can be as beneficial as visiting a psychiatrist. Most people talk affectionately to their pets, and treat them lovingly. This, apparently, is psychologically good for both animal and owner. Even the simple act of stroking a pet can lower blood pressure and heart rate.

Another way in which a dog can be man's best friend!

THE FRIENDSHIP BOOK

SUNDAY—APRIL 10.

THE meek will he guide in judgment: and the meek will he teach his way.

MONDAY—APRIL 11.

ABOUT a year before his death, Professor Petain, who had served many years as a medical missionary in Africa, was called to a man suffering from severe bronchitis. The physician asked to be left alone with his patient and proceeded to listen carefully to his chest, asking him to count aloud slowly.

Waiting behind the door for the verdict, the anxious wife was surprised how long the consultation seemed to be taking. At last she opened the door and went in to see what was the matter.

She found the overworked doctor asleep on her husband's chest, while the latter was steadily counting and had nearly reached 500!

TUESDAY—APRIL 12.

A FIFTEEN-YEAR-OLD boy was at Mount Clemens Station, a small out-of-the-way place in Ohio, chatting with the station-master, when the latter's little girl wandered on to the line in front of an approaching train.

The teenager immediately dashed forward and swept her to safety. The child's father could not reward the youth with money, but he rewarded him in a much more valuable way. He taught him telegraphy, and before very long the youth became an acknowledged expert, known to us all for many other inventions—Thomas Alva Edison.

GOOD FRIENDS

ROBERT LOUIS STEVENSON is still remembered for his fine adventure stories including " Treasure Island " and " Kidnapped ". His memorial tablet in St. Giles Cathedral, Edinburgh, depicts him reclining on a couch, pen in one hand, paper in another, bringing to mind the gallant struggles of the man who fought life-long illness and who yet could say:

" Keep your eyes open to your mercies. The man who forgets to be grateful has fallen asleep in life." And also: " Faith is to believe in God and if you believe in God, where is there any room for terror?"

THURSDAY—APRIL 14.

YEHUDI MENUHIN, the world-famous violinist, has said that real satisfaction in any achievement comes when a person " lifts his gaze to the thing that makes his work bigger than himself."

You might think that he would illustrate this from the world of music, but not so. Instead he tells how he was once taken on a conducted tour of a restaurant kitchen, and he paused to watch the giant dish-washing machine in action. It was being tended by a Negro kitchen assistant who told him, " This is the most important job in the place. If we don't get the dishes real clean and keep the water hot enough to kill all the germs, folk will get sick."

Which of us, I wonder, would have plumped for the dish-washer as holding the most important job in the kitchen? Yet how right he was; and how elevated is the humblest job when we see it in terms of responsibility and vocation.

FRIDAY—APRIL 15.

A FARNBOROUGH schoolteacher asked a seven-year-old boy during a religious education class, " Why do we say ' Amen ' at the end of our prayers?"

After some thought the boy replied, " It's a special way of saying ' over and out ' to God."

Which, when you stop to think, is a lovely way of saying " So be it "—and then trustfully leaving it all to Him.

SATURDAY—APRIL 16.

ELISABETH SCHWARZKOPF, the great soprano, spends much of her time nowadays teaching young singers in places as far apart as Paris and San Francisco. In an interview recently she said, " There is so much talent about, and I feel so privileged that I am able to pass on what lessons I have learned."

Few of us have the gifts or the opportunities of an Elisabeth Schwarzkopf. Yet, within our own limitations, we all have this privilege of being able to share with others the things we have learned from life. Don't let's keep good things to ourselves—whether it's a recipe we have enjoyed, a good book we have read, a prayer that has helped us, or anything else which has brought us joy. Better to pass it on and enrich the common stock of happiness.

SUNDAY—APRIL 17.

WHILE the earth remaineth, seedtime and harvest, and cold and heat, and summer and winter, and day and night shall not cease.

THE FRIENDSHIP BOOK

KATE KELLY of Merseyside is a very busy woman. She has two lively children of her own at home, and a lot more at school where she's a full-time teacher. So there's not a lot of day left at the end of her work. But Kate makes a point of setting aside a certain time each week for letter writing. As she says, " Even if I can spare only half an hour it's time that is never wasted. There's always someone who could do with a few cheerful words."

She's quite right, of course. We all know it to be true. But how many of these letters we write in our head ever get as far as the notepaper?

Have you written one lately?

SHEILA, who is nine years old, was busy at her homework, clearly engrossed in what she was doing. Looking over her shoulder her father enquired what she was writing so industriously about.

" I am writing a report about the world," was the rather surprising reply.

" My word! That's a bit of a tall order, isn't it?" he said.

" Oh, I don't know," said Sheila. " There are three of us working on it in my class."

Which presumably should make it easy! Those of us who have contact with children must often be struck by their sheer exuberance and confidence, and some of it must surely brush off on us. No wonder a friend of mine says, " Having grandchildren doesn't make you feel old. It keeps you young!"

A BUSINESS man who was also a great art lover had built up over the years, by dint of much sacrifice, a quite considerable art collection. One of his rather worldly friends visited him one day and cast his eyes over the pictures. " My," he said, " what a lot of money you could get if you sold all these!"

The collector looked puzzled. " But," he said, " if I had a lot of money, these are the things I would buy!"

His friend thought of riches in terms of money, the art lover in terms of things which brought him joy and satisfaction. It is for each of us to discover the things that really matter to us—then are we truly wealthy.

T HIS is one of the most beautiful prayers I know:

" My Lord God, I have no idea where I am going. I do not see the road ahead of me. I cannot know for certain where it will end. Nor do I really know myself, and the fact that I think I am following Your will does not mean that I am actually doing so. But I believe that the desire to please You does in fact please You, and I hope that I will never do anything apart from that desire.

" I know that if I do this You will lead me by the right road though I may know nothing about it. Therefore will I trust You always though I may seem to be lost and in the shadow of death. I will not fear, for You are ever with me, and You will never leave me to face my perils alone."

Amen.

WOODLANDS

Trees have moods for every season,
Changing beauty, fresh displayed.
Could there be a better reason
All year round to seek their shade?

FRIDAY—APRIL 22.

NEAR the swift flowing River Swale in North Yorkshire stands ruined Easby Abbey, once the home of monks and still a peaceful spot not far from historic Richmond.

Alongside is the tiny church of Easby, and in its porch, I am told, are these encouraging words:

Here a man shall be free from the noise and hurryings of this life.

God give you rest and make your heart the subject of His care,

God give you love, a Gift received from Him without Compare,

God keep you, friend.

What a lovely welcome!

SATURDAY—APRIL 23.

IN a famous painting, " The Annunciation ", by the Florentine artist, Fra Filippo Lippi, you will notice, if you look carefully, a hand right at the top of the picture, reaching down. I am told that this is the artist's way of saying that heaven is very close to earth, that God " has a hand in " the ordinary events of our lives.

For those who hold this simple faith there truly is a " heaven on earth " and with the poet they can say,

Earth's crammed with heaven
And every common bush afire with God.

SUNDAY—APRIL 24.

REMEMBER not the sins of my youth, nor my transgressions: according to thy mercy remember thou me for thy goodness' sake, O Lord.

NEARLY 150 years ago, a small girl was playing with her hoop in the streets of a Derbyshire village when she heard the sound of shouting and jeering. Along the street came a policeman holding a poorly dressed, hungry-looking man whom he had arrested. It seemed a great joke to the rabble who followed—but not the small girl. Her eyes filled with sympathy, she put her hoop over her shoulder and marched alongside him all the way to the police station.

It was not the last time she marched side by side with the prisoner, the poor, the unfortunate—for that little girl was Catherine Mumford who later was to become wife and helpmate of William Booth, the founder of the Salvation Army.

A LITTLE old lady was struggling to get on the train with a case almost as big as herself.

" Allow me to lift that on for you," offered a stranger, but he couldn't because she clung on to the case handle.

" Let go, and I'll put the case on for you," he urged her, but still she clung tight.

The guard blew his whistle and the man boarded the train, only to turn and see the old lady still trying in vain to lift up her case. In a last bid to help he leaned out. " Let go," he said, and at last she did.

A lot of us are like that old lady. We cling tightly to our worries, anxieties and other burdens, when life would be so much easier if only we would let others share them.

BRAVE SHOW

The tulip army's on parade
Beneath the castle wall;
In colours gay they greet the day,
Erect and proud and tall.
Kings and queens of long ago
Were never granted such a show.

THE FRIENDSHIP BOOK

THE other day I overheard someone complaining at great length. She was telling her friend that she had so much to do that she did not know where to start. And the more she delayed starting, the more there was to do, so it was a growing problem.

It reminded me of the story of the centipede who lay down in the road and gave up trying to walk. He was afraid in case he used the wrong foot first and tripped over, so he didn't use any of his feet at all.

THE 19th century American writer, Oliver Wendell Holmes, once said: " I am a regular church-goer. I should go for various reasons even if I did not love it, but I am fortunate enough to find pleasure in the midst of devout multitudes, whether I can accept all their creed or not. For I find there is in the corner of my heart a little plant called reverence which wants to be watered about once a week."

Whether we use Wendell Holmes's method or some other, we certainly need to do something to keep the plant of reverence alive. It often seems a weakly growth in the world about us—whether it be reverence for truth, for beauty, for other people, their rights, their property, let alone for God, His laws, His Day, His holy Book.

We may not feel ourselves very important or influential, but if we can do something to keep the plant of reverence watered in our hearts we may be doing more than we dream possible to make the world a better and happier place in which to live.

MY friend James Murray helped me to stack logs from the dead tree that I had cut down. He is not a particularly robust man, yet he carried heavier logs than I could manage.

" I'm sure I'm not doing my share, yet my back is shouting the opposite," I said, rubbing the aches.

" You'll manage fine if you bend your knees to pick up the heavy logs. You've been bending your back," James corrected me.

I watched him a moment and saw how his bent legs took the strain while his back remained straight.

" Remember, it's not what you carry but the way that you carry it that matters," James added, striding off with yet another load.

When you think about it, that is true of all life's burdens, isn't it? Often it is not the weight that drags us down. What really matters is how we handle our troubles. Do we do it with bitterness and resentment, or with courage, hope and cheerfulness?

The right attitude makes the burden lighter.

SATURDAY—APRIL 30.

SOME time ago, a teacher said to his class of boys: " I want you to tell me one thing of great importance that we have now which we did not have a hundred years ago." He expected the answers to be aeroplanes, motor cars, television, or radio. Only one boy put up his hand. " I know, sir."

" Well, my lad, what is it?"

" Why—ME, sir."

And of course he was right!

MAY

SUNDAY—MAY 1.

TEACH me thy way, O Lord, and lead me in a plain path, because of mine enemies.

MONDAY—MAY 2.

WHEN Joanna was four years old she loved helping. After watching the Lady of the House ironing, she said, " I want to help you."

" All right, you spread the hankies and dish towels out ready for me," the Lady of the House suggested.

" No, I want to iron," Joanna replied, and became tearful when told the iron was " too hot and dangerous."

Then, when I was mowing the lawn, she asked if she could help me.

" Well, will you please pick up the grass cuttings on the path?" I asked.

" No, I want to push the mower," Joanna insisted.

She refused to do the tasks that she was big enough to handle, but insisted on attempting those for which she was too small!

Thinking about this after she had gone home, it struck me how often I am like that myself. I neglect small things such as sending a get-well card to a sick friend, or a phone-call to someone housebound—I am too busy planning to do bigger things the next day. How much better if I remembered that a loving deed today is worth far more than the great achievements I *intend* to do tomorrow!

JOURNEY'S END

Is there anything better than an open road
And a sun that bakes you brown?
Yes, there's the sound of a friendly voice:
" Welcome—do sit down!"

THE FRIENDSHIP BOOK

DURING an election campaign a candidate was urging his followers to become, not just involved, but committed. Someone in the audience asked what the difference was.

The speaker hesitated for a moment and then he said, " Well, I guess it's like eggs and bacon. The eggs are involved, but the pig is committed!"

Some people never seem to be involved in anything outside their own personal interests. But if we really want a happy, satisfying life we need something to which we feel ourselves to be deeply committed—it may be a good cause, a charity, a club to which we belong, a church, a hobby—it does not much matter as long as it is something which really engrosses us, for engrossed people are never bored and unhappy.

NEW to me is the story of the man who spent most of his life longing to go to heaven. When he died, an angel took him on a kind of conducted tour. He showed him majestic mountains and rushing streams, noble forests and flowery meadows. There were children laughing and playing and the sound of music everywhere. One glad and beautiful sight after another was shown to him.

How wonderful!" he exclaimed. " So this is heaven!"

" No," replied the angel. " This is the world in which you lived and never saw!"

A reminder that we should always keep our eyes open to the beauties and wonders around us. Let's enjoy them!

I HAD met a school friend of many years ago and we were discussing, I need hardly tell you, other friends of those days.

Two of these were sisters. Doris used to be very good-looking while her sister Jean was considered plain.

You can imagine my surprise when my friend said, " It's Jean who is the pretty one now."

I couldn't understand this till she explained.

" Yes " she said. " Jean has done so many good things in her life that it shows in her face."

Could any woman ever have a nicer tribute paid to her?

GREAT men are often thought of as being so engrossed with great affairs that they have little time for lesser things—even sometimes the simple courtesies of life. An incident between the President of the U.S.A., F. D. Roosevelt, and Winston Churchill, during World War II, gives the lie to that.

Churchill had been staying with Roosevelt at the White House and afterwards he told a companion that the President had been very friendly. " He must have noticed the candle by my bed, because there was a small lighted candle on the luncheon table by my place to light my cigar."

That one great man should give attention to a detail of another's comfort and that the other should notice it says a good deal about greatness.

Thought for others and the recognition of others' thought for us—this is a way of " greatness " within the scope of us all.

THE FRIENDSHIP BOOK

I LIKE the old tale of the preacher who was urging his congregation to repent.

"Unless ye turn from your wicked ways," he thundered, "you'll be lost—as sure as I'm going to squash this wasp with the hymn-book I hold in my hand."

Down came the book, but the wasp rose just in time, and the book descended harmlessly.

"Ah, well, friends," said the preacher, "maybe it's the Almighty's will that you should have one more chance!"

THOU hast also given me the shield of thy salvation: and thy gentleness hath made me great.

A FRIEND was looking at his son's school report and was not altogether satisfied with his position in the class.

"Fourteenth," he said, frowning. "That means that you are half-way down the class."

"Well," came the reply, "I'm half-way *up* as well, amn't I?"

I think he would be the sort of boy who, if he was half-way through a packet of sweets, wouldn't say sadly, "It's half-empty." He would say, "It is still half-full!"

What a difference it would make to our happiness if we could learn to look gratefully at what we *have* instead of bemoaning what we have not.

OLD FRIEND

Of course we need to be modern,
  Move with the times, as they say;
Such wonderful things are invented
  Each and every day.

But still they are not forgotten,
  The ways that were quiet and slow;
Just look at the welcome waiting
  For a friend of long ago!

TUESDAY—MAY 10.

DID they use nicknames in Biblical times, I wonder? This thought struck me when I read for the first time in a modern translation of the Bible some words in the fourth chapter of the Acts of the Apostles: " . . . Joseph, a Levite born in Cyprus, whom the apostles called Barnabas (which means ' One who Encourages.')"

It really does look as though " Barnabas " was a nickname given to Joseph. Nicknames can sometimes be given cruelly, sometimes humorously and sometimes, as here, because of some endearing quality. Could we desire any better name ourselves? Encouragement is something we all need and something we can all give.

Someone once said, " The best way to knock a chip off a fellow's shoulder is by patting him on the back." How true!

WEDNESDAY—MAY 11.

MRS M. Riley of Oulton Broad, Suffolk, sent me these appealing lines which she has entitled " Essentials ".

When you have a key, you need a lock
  In which the key will fit.
When you have a lock, you need a door
  In which the lock will sit.
When you have a door, you need a wall
  In which the door will stand.
When you have four walls, you need a roof
  To make your house look grand.
When you have your house just right for you,
  You can settle and never roam,
But with all these things you need a mate
  To make your house a home.

THE FRIENDSHIP BOOK

THERE was, many years ago, in a Yorkshire village, an old character with a horse and cart who ran a light haulage service to the neighbouring towns. Painted on the back of the cart was a notice which said that his service was in operation: "TUESDAYS AND THURSDAYS (D.V.) — SATURDAYS (D.V. or Not)."

We may smile at that, but I wonder whether, if we are honest with ourselves, that does not represent something of our own thoughts at times. In the Lord's Prayer we ask that God's will may be done by us—but I reckon that what we are really praying sometimes is that our will may be done by God—a very different thing!

SCIENTISTS now agree that the power of touch is a force to be reckoned with. But haven't you and I always known that a loving touch can soothe away pain, and take the place of words?

A mother needs to touch her new baby frequently; and a toddler depends on the warmth of human contact for its survival. Even independent teenagers appreciate the emotional support shown by a quick hug or a peck on the cheek. And no matter how secure an elderly person may seem, a friendly arm around his or her shoulder may mean the difference between hope and despair.

Next time you get the chance to shake someone by the hand, don't miss the opportunity. To offer or receive the hand of friendship is a beautiful thing. This world would be a far more peaceful and loving place, if only we all " kept in touch ".

THE FRIENDSHIP BOOK

SATURDAY—MAY 14.

THERE are so many ways to say " Thank you "
When words are too hard to express.
A silent touch on a shoulder,
A hand that in comfort we press;
Eye meeting eye and a nod of the head
Flash a message there's no need to guess.
So many ways a " Thank you " is sent
Without words, yet we know what is meant.

SUNDAY—MAY 15.

THE Lord shall judge the people: judge me, O Lord, according to my righteousness, and according to mine integrity that is in me.

MONDAY—MAY 16.

THE visit of a fair nearby reminded me of the story of a showman going the round of the fairgrounds with nothing more exciting to show than a stuffed crocodile. However, he tried to make his exhibit sound as attractive as possible by standing at the door of his tent and shouting, " Roll up, Roll up! Come and see the amazing stuffed crocodile, measuring 18 feet from the tip of its nose to the tip of its tail, and 18 feet from the tip of its tail to the tip of its nose, making, in all, ladies and gentlemen, no less than 36 feet!"

I'm afraid that is the way that sometimes we measure our troubles, measuring them, measuring them again, adding the two together and making them sound much more formidable than they really are!

If we are going to do any double-measuring, let's do it with our blessings.

THE FRIENDSHIP BOOK

A HEAVY lorry had broken down outside a church. The driver tinkered with the engine, with apparently no success, and was just about to express himself forcibly when his mate jerked his thumb in the direction of a Wayside Pulpit notice-board.

It read: " Keep your temper: Nobody wants it."

A broad smile slowly spread over the face of the driver, and he again resumed his attempts to find the fault. In a few moments he had succeeded, and off went the vehicle to its destination.

Perhaps keeping our temper may not always enable us to rectify a mechanical fault, but it certainly creates a more hopeful and positive attitude.

PHILLIPS BROOKS was a well-known American preacher last century who won wide acclaim for his sermons and his scholarship. Probably no greater tribute could be paid to him than that in a paragraph which appeared in a Boston newspaper: " It was a dull, rainy day when things looked dark and glowering, but Phillips Brooks came down through Newspaper Row and all was bright."

We can be sure that his infectious, cheerful spirit would be remembered long after his eloquent sermons were forgotten. We may not share Phillips Brooks's gifts of oratory and learning, but it is not beyond the power of most of us to radiate a little cheerfulness and optimism. This is as much a ministry as preaching.

THURSDAY—MAY 19.

I WAS staying with a friend one weekend and had the luxury of a breakfast tray in bed. One member of the family was Dixie, a lovely golden retriever dog, who, having decided I was an acceptable guest came to visit me while I was eating.

There was a banana on my tray, as yet uneaten, and this Dixie eyed thoughtfully. Then he trotted out of the room, down the stairs and into the kitchen. A moment later he returned carrying his prized bone which he laid gently on the bed, then, looking me straight in the eye and wagging his tail—speaking eloquently if ever a dog spoke—he equally gently removed the banana.

I learnt afterwards that Dixie was very fond of bananas. I can't say I'm particularly fond of bones, but to him it was certainly a fair exchange!

FRIDAY—MAY 20.

IN the early days of crossword puzzles, when clues were very much more straightforward than they are today, a man had completed one puzzle all except one four-letter word, the clue for which was " A shop's receptacle for keeping money ". Finally, he gave up and waited for the solution to be published the following day.

The answer was " till ", and of course there was nothing remarkable about that—except that the gentleman concerned had worked for over 40 years with a firm that manufactured cash tills!

It is odd what a " blind spot " we can have about the familiar. How little we notice the things about us! The world is full of beauty and wonder—if we will only look.

THE FRIENDSHIP BOOK

WE often hear of young folk who flash into prominence and then burn out because they don't develop any further. Melvyn Douglas, as a young man, made a name for himself in romantic roles in the cinema. When that time passed he turned to playing character parts and carved out a new career.

Asked how he had succeeded in making this very different use of his talents he said briefly: " I got better."

Three words which, I am sure, concealed a mountain of hard work.

WHAT is a man profited, if he shall gain the whole world, and lose his own soul?

ARNOLD BENNETT, the writer, was intrigued when a publisher he knew kept singing the praises of his secretary. One day when Bennett and the secretary were alone he asked her, " What is the secret of this wonderful efficiency of yours? Your employer is always talking about it."

" It is not my secret," smiled the secretary. " It is *his*." And she went on to explain that whatever duty she performed, however small it was, he never failed to acknowledge it and thank her for it. This encouraged her to give of her very best, whatever she was doing.

A few words of gratitude and encouragement *do* bring out the best in other people. Just give it a try and you'll see.

HEALING

Oh, there's magic in the wind's song,
There's healing in the hill,
And peace comes gently stealing
Where the water's never still.

TUESDAY—MAY 24.

MRS NANCY SMITH, 41 Eglinton Crescent, Troon, has been in a wheelchair for years.

She tells me of an incident that she always recalls when she feels she needs something to smile about.

She'd been confined to the house for days because of pouring rain. So when the sun broke through, she hurried to get on her coat. She went through the house, laboriously snibbing windows, locking doors, etc., and made her way to the garage to get into her car. Alas, the rain had swollen the wooden doors and because of the meagre strength in her arms, Nancy couldn't get them to budge.

Exhausted and disappointed, she returned to the house. After sitting a while to recover, she made a cup of tea. Usually that cheers her up, but it didn't seem enough on this occasion. So she lifted her Bible and let it fall open at random, to see if it would turn up some message of solace for her.

When she saw what the book had fallen open at, she burst out laughing. It was " Lamentations "!

WEDNESDAY—MAY 25.

A TEACHER friend told me once of a schoolboy writing in an essay: " Nostalgia is what makes Mum cry when she talks of the good times she had when she was a girl."

That is certainly how looking back affects some people. However, Joyce Grenfell, who in her life gave pleasure to so many people, looked at things very differently. In a letter to a friend she wrote: " Isn't it odd the way people get sad about happy times in the past, just because they are past. I *go on* enjoying them."

THURSDAY—MAY 26.

THE other Saturday evening I was walking along the road when I noticed my friend the librarian mowing the grass on his neighbour's lawn.

This seemed rather odd, but when I stopped and spoke to him it turned out that it hadn't taken him as long as he had expected to mow his own grass, so he thought he would mow Fred's too. Fred was away for the weekend so it would be a nice surprise for him when he came home.

"And do you know," said the librarian, "I hated mowing my own grass, but I have actually enjoyed doing Fred's. Would you believe that?"

Yes, I do!

FRIDAY—MAY 27.

THE Bishop of Reading, the Right Rev. Eric Wild, told this amusing story. He was once visiting a family and while the vicar was out of the room the small daughter of the house asked him, "Can you please tell me something that Daddy can't understand?"

"I'll certainly try," said the Bishop.

"Well," enquired the child innocently, "Daddy can't understand how you ever became a Bishop!"

SATURDAY—MAY 28.

DALE CARNEGIE, the popular writer of many books, once came out with this thought-provoking comment: "You can make more friends in two months by becoming interested in other people than you can in two years by trying to get other people interested in you."

THE FRIENDSHIP BOOK

LORD, I have loved the habitation of thy house, and the place where thine honour dwelleth.

HENRY FREDERIC AMIEL was a 19th-century Professor of Moral Philosophy at Geneva. He also kept a diary for over 40 years, and in it is this lovely passage: " I find a charm in the rain—it makes colours that are otherwise dull seem like soft velvet, and makes the flat-looking tones more tender. The landscape is like a face that has been weeping; maybe it is less beautiful, but it is certainly more expressive."

Next time it's too wet to go out, just ponder those words of Professor Amiel . . .

ONE of the greatly loved and influential ministers of a former generation was J.P. Struthers of Greenock. Many who perhaps forgot his moving sermons never forgot some of the simple acts of kindness which formed so great a part of his ministry.

One of them was to gather flowers from his garden and make them up into little posies which he laid along the top of his garden wall by the roadside. Those who saw them knew that they were there for them to take and to give to others—children to their mothers, visitors to the sick and elderly, lads to their sweethearts.

How much happier a place the world would be if more of us learned to give and share out kindness and a little beauty.

JUNE

WEDNESDAY—JUNE 1.

ON a hot summer's day, stand near a bee hive and listen. Keep very quiet and still, and gradually you will become aware of a persistent sibilant note, and a gentle burring sound. The fanner-bees are at work. It is their job to keep the hive sweet and fresh, and a current of fresh air circulating in the hive for coolness and for purity. They will be standing inside, their heads lowered, facing the centre of the hive. Their wings will be moving so rapidly, that if you could see in, you would think they were surrounded on either side by a grey mist.

These bees draw out the bad air through one side of the hive while pure air is sucked in the other. If you lit a match and held it near the hive entrance, the draught they cause would blow it out! Those tiny wings *moving in unison* can make a draught strong enough to blow out a match—incredible, isn't it?

If there were enough fanner-bee Christians as thorough at their job as these bees, what a difference it would make! Wouldn't the world be a sweeter and fresher place?

THURSDAY—JUNE 2.

WHEN he was the Papal Nuncio in Paris, Pope John XXIII was asked about women who were presented to him wearing dresses cut rather low. His reply was illuminating: " I don't look at them. Neither do other men. They are too busy looking at me to see what my reaction is!"

THE FRIENDSHIP BOOK

FRIDAY—JUNE 3.

I WAS a patient," wrote a famous poet, " in the old Infirmary of Edinburgh. I had heard vaguely of Lister, and went there as a sort of forlorn hope on the chance of saving my foot. The great surgeon received me, as he did everybody, with the greatest kindness, and for 20 months I lay in one or other ward of the old place under his care. It was a desperate business, but he saved my foot, and here I am."

The poet, William Ernest Henley, was telling an audience of the circumstances in which he wrote the poem which begins:

I am the master of my fate,
I am the captain of my soul . . .

SATURDAY—JUNE 4.

WAY back in 1941 a well-known Methodist minister said: " When you get fed up with present-day happenings, go out into the lanes and the fields, and listen and look at the things of Nature. There is no hurry in that world—that is why I am a dodderer. I lose all sense of time when I'm in the country, I forget the speed of machinery. To be a dodderer is a lost art these days, one that we should recapture."

His words still make plenty of sense. The speaker was the Rev. George Bramwell Evans — better known as " Romany " of the BBC and of Children's Hour.

SUNDAY—JUNE 5.

IF any man come after me, let him deny himself, and take up his cross, and follow me.

MONDAY—JUNE 6.

WHAT is a saint? I rather like the definition I once heard: " saints are sinners who did not give in."

Years ago a curate in West Yorkshire told the story of a small boy who was taken to look round an ancient church by his father who had been trying to explain what a saint was. Together they gazed up at a stained glass window depicting a saint, but the little lad was not at all impressed until suddenly the sun shone through the window, illuminating the jewelled colours and making it " come alive ".

" Oh, now I see," cried the boy. " A saint is someone the sun shines through."

TUESDAY—JUNE 7.

THE late Dr. William Barclay told the story of a London taxi driver who had to take a test involving knowledge of the shortest route between any two points in the city. He studied the maps till he knew them by heart—but he failed the test.

In answer to a question about the quickest route from one place to another he gave what clearly was the shortest on the map. It would, however, have meant taking his taxi down a long flight of steps and through a passage wide enough only for pedestrians!

Short cuts are not always what they seem. While we should be grateful for the inventions which have helped to reduce the labour and drudgery of life, we should always keep in mind that most of the things worth having come to us through patience and effort. Don't let's be deluded by life's " short cuts ".

THE FRIENDSHIP BOOK

MY little friend Joanna had been practising running for weeks. " I mean to win the silver cup," she told me.

On Sports Day I watched her speed down the track well ahead of the other girls. Surely I was about to see her fulfil her ambition. But even as I thought it—disaster! Joanna stumbled and fell on to her knees.

But was it disaster? In a flash she was on her feet again and on she raced to win the coveted cup. When I congratulated her I mentioned the fall that nearly cost her the race, and that had certainly grazed her knees.

" I didn't stop to look at my knees, I just kept my eyes on the winning post," she grinned.

Wise girl! She has already learned that she will go much further in life if she refuses to allow tumbles, mistakes or other setbacks to prevent her from reaching her goals.

A WELL-KNOWN TV personality was driving along Barnet High Street when he was flagged down by a policeman on the pavement.

" Haven't I seen you somewhere before, sir?" asked the constable.

" Well ", said the driver, " I wouldn't be at all surprised, officer, you see . . . "

But before he could finish, the constable collected his thoughts. " I've got it," he said. " Tottenham Court—five years ago—careless driving. Good morning, sir."

Richard Baker, BBC news-reader, drove carefully on, chuckling to himself . . .

IN the Eskimo language, believe it or not, there is no word which corresponds with our word "joy ." So when one of the agents of the Bible Society was translating a well-known passage in St Luke's Gospel, he didn't know what to put.

Then he saw one of the husky dogs enjoying himself immensely with a bone.

After discussing the matter with an Eskimo friend he wrote down, "There shall be tail-wagging in the presence of God over one sinner that repenteth."

YEARS ago, in many parts of the country, it was the custom, and a mark of house-wifely pride, to scour the front doorsteps and sometimes the pavement with what was known as Cam or Donkey Stone. This is a commodity which has now almost gone out of existence but there are older housewives who would dearly like to get hold of some again.

One woman in Yorkshire said she would like to scour her cellar floor. Asked why she would bother scouring part of her house that her neighbours would never see, she replied, " You have got to do it for your own respect. I always believed in putting my right side inside, not my right side outside."

Well, there's a lot in what she says—and not only for scouring floors.

BE still, and know that I am God.

COUNTRY JOY

There is nothing so rare as a Summer's day
When the sky is blue and the sun shines bright,
And the stream runs cool on its lazy way
And the whole wide world is exactly right;
Oh, then is there anything else so sweet
As God's green grass beneath your feet?

MONDAY—JUNE 13.

"FIT to be Gates of Paradise " was the opinion of Michelangelo when he saw the beautiful doors Ghiberti had made for the Baptistry of San Giovanni in Florence. This was the ultimate in praise from a great artist for the work of an unknown craftsman.

Ghiberti had been a young man when he heard that plans would be considered for these important doors. Inspired by the challenge, he submitted designs, and to his joy his designs were accepted, despite the keen competition.

The magnificent doors became his life's work—the first one took him 21 years to complete, the second 27 years, and he was an old man by the time the work was finished.

TUESDAY—JUNE 14.

"WHERE did it come from?" little Joanna once asked. She was down on her hands and knees gazing at a solitary daisy growing out of my garden path.

" It pushed up through that crack," I explained, but Joanna remained unsatisfied. " But *how*, Uncle? How did it get there?"

I tried to explain about seeds and roots but the daisy's deepest secrets remained hidden—from me as well as from Joanna.

Carl Linnaeus, the great Swedish botanist, said that there was enough mystery in a handful of moss to give one a lifetime's study. In the light of that statement, how could I ever explain the hows and whys of a daisy to a child?

But I'm grateful to her for opening my eyes afresh to the wonder of it all.

THE FRIENDSHIP BOOK

I LIKE the story of the small boy who was in hospital when it was visited by a special deputation from the Hospital Board. The sister of each ward conducted the visitors round and in the group was a duchess. It was she who greeted the small boy cheerily, " Hello, sonny."

" Hello, Missis," he said.

Sister was embarrassed. " You shouldn't say that," she protested. " You should say, ' Your Grace!' "

At once the small boy piped up, " For what we are about to receive may the Lord make us truly thankful."

OLD Janie had been a pillar of the church for many years and the building was crowded for her funeral service. One of the tributes which the minister paid to her in his address I shall never forget. He had spoken of the various offices she had held in the church and then he said, " I remember visiting Janie one hot summer afternoon. She was always hospitable but that afternoon she greeted me at the door with the words, ' Tea's brewed! I saw you pushing your bicycle up that long hill to my house and I thought, ' That good man will need some refreshment when he gets here,' so I put the kettle on right away, and it's all ready for you!' "

I shall remember that when I have forgotten Janie's official positions in the church. To help people when we can—that's good; but to anticipate their needs, that really is true compassion.

FRIDAY—JUNE 17.

I WAS talking to my friend the Librarian the other day. He has problems with his nerves, and he was telling me about one Monday morning when he had felt particularly low.

Suddenly it was as if a voice spoke to him: " In quietness and confidence shall be your strength." He knew the verse well enough—Isaiah 30, verse 15. Now he believed it, and in a very short time his spirits lifted and he felt much better.

Next day, he visited a house-bound lady who was very worried about herself, and because he knew that verse had worked for him—he commended it to her, too.

" In quietness and confidence shall be your strength." Beautiful words with a beautiful message.

SATURDAY—JUNE 18.

THE Rev. Arthur B. Jordan had a son at college. His boy was about to take his final examinations, and naturally father asked his son to let him know as soon as possible how he got on.

A few days later, Mr Jordan received a telegram. It read: " Hymn 254, verse five, last two lines."

Looking up the reference in *Hymns Ancient and Modern,* he read: " Sorrow vanquished, labour ended, Jordan passed ".

SUNDAY—JUNE 19.

UNTO man he said, Behold, the fear of the Lord, that is wisdom; and to depart from evil is understanding.

THE FRIENDSHIP BOOK

MONDAY—JUNE 20.

A REGULAR commuter, accustomed to an extra forty winks on the train, always produced his ticket automatically if an inspector asked to see it. Often he hardly opened his eyes.

One morning, as he dozed peacefully, he felt a gentle but persistent shaking of his shoulder. With half-open eyes, he reached into his pocket and held out his season ticket. Suddenly he heard his wife's voice muttering in his ear, and woke up with a start.

It was Sunday morning and the collection was being taken in church . . .

TUESDAY—JUNE 21.

IN the Town Hall at High Wycombe is the Oak Room which has a window commemorating Hannah Ball, born in Buckinghamshire on March 13th, 1734.

She it was who in 1769 began one of England's first known Sunday Schools, an informal gathering which met every Sunday and Monday. In one of her letters to the Rev. John Wesley, she described the children as " a wild little company, but they seem willing to be instructed." Wesley replied: " I am glad that you remain at High Wycombe. That is undoubtedly your place. You have a large field in which to exercise all the graces and gifts that God has given to you."

Hannah Ball remained Superintendent of that Sunday School until her death in 1792. Her example in initiating Sunday Schools inspired others, notably Robert Raikes, one of the founders of the English Sunday School movement.

WEDNESDAY—JUNE 22.

A SMALL boy was once asked to tell a story from Aesop's Fables in his own words. He picked the one about the fox coming across a goat stranded in a well.

The fox looked down at the goat and said, " I'm so sorry."

" Sorry!" the goat replied. " Stop being sorry and *do* something."

This tale still applies as much today as in Aesop's time!

In its prime, Kirkstall Abbey, West Yorkshire, housed dozens of monks and lay brothers—all kept busy. Yet whenever a beggar knocked at the gatehouse of the Abbey—now part of the Abbey House Museum—the porter would cry " Thank God!" because once again the monks could be of help to a human being in distress.

THURSDAY—JUNE 23.

THOMAS CARLYLE, the great 19th century scholar, once stopped in the middle of a busy street. At the risk of being knocked down by a cab he bent down and picked something up out of the mud. He cleaned it, then left it on the pavement.

" It was only a crust of bread," he said, " but my mother taught me never to waste anything. I'm sure the sparrows or a hungry dog will get nourishment from it."

In days of hardship and shortages it is more important than ever not to waste. And this does not apply only to material things. Hours and minutes are precious too. And what about words? We can waste them—or we can use them to comfort and cheer, to encourage and inspire.

THE FRIENDSHIP BOOK

DURING the Second World War, Lord Moran was physician to Winston Churchill and travelled with him on arduous and sometimes perilous journeys round the world. He kept a diary, extracts from which were later published in his book: *Winston Churchill: The Struggle for Survival.*

He tells in one place how Churchill asked him, " Is much known about worry, Charles?" and then went on (as so often, without waiting for an answer!), " It helps to write down half a dozen things which are worrying me. Two of them, say, disappear; about two, nothing can be done, so it's no use worrying; and two perhaps can be settled."

There may be few ways in which we can emulate the great man, but this could be one of them. Try it!

SATURDAY—JUNE 25.

THE Rev. McEwen Lawson once said, " There should be a Society for the Prevention of Cruelty to Words! One of the chief sufferers is the word ' love.' The trouble is that in English we have only one label for very different kinds of love. We say ' I love nougat,' ' I love Beethoven,' ' I love my child,' ' I love the rhumba,' ' I love Skye,' ' I love God.' "

I suppose that one of the great difficulties for many of us is when we are told that we should " love one another," that, in effect, we should love everybody! I think we *do* need other words here. Perhaps we could say we wished them well instead, and if we wished everybody well, what a lot of the world's problems would be solved!

HEAVENWARDS

The men of old who built each lofty spire
Meant them to be seen from all around,
Reminding us to raise our vision higher
Than day to day affairs upon the ground.

THE FRIENDSHIP BOOK

LORD, thou hast heard the desire of the humble: thou wilt prepare their heart, thou wilt cause thine ear to hear.

MONDAY—JUNE 27.

MARGARET McLEOD asked her husband to call at the local chemist's shop to collect a photograph of their baby son, aged just five months.

Apparently there was some mix-up with the photographs, but Margaret didn't hear about it until she visited the chemist's herself a few days later. The smiling assistant told her that she'd shown Mr McLeod a photograph of a baby and asked if it was theirs. He had looked at it for a moment and then said: " No, that's not him—our wallpaper's different!"

TUESDAY—JUNE 28.

JIMMY FIRTH was a young sailor from London, and about 200 years ago he brought home a plant from Brazil. His mother cultivated it and later a cutting from the plant was presented to the Royal Botanic Gardens at Kew. Commercial nurserymen from Hammersmith cultivated it, propagated it, and raised many more new ones, so that today there are well over 1,000 garden varieties on the market!

That little flower which Captain Firth had brought home to his mother was the genesis of all the beautiful bell-shaped fuchsias now common all over the country, the harvest from that simple little kindness of a young sailor to his mother.

THE FRIENDSHIP BOOK

IRENE LAURE, a French resistance leader, tells the story of a small boy who asked his parents, " How do wars begin?" His father began a rather complicated account of political and economic factors and his mother felt that this was all too difficult for her little son, so she broke in saying, " Let me explain." She started to try but Father soon broke in impatiently and an angry argument developed. The little boy was very frightened and cried out, " Stop! Stop! Now I know how wars begin!"

It is a humbling thought to know that we often play our part in the world's unrest—but there is the other side, too: we can play our part in the world's peace.

THE American writer, Irving Kristel, once said, " Being frustrated is disagreeable, but the real disasters of life begin when you get what you want!"

This, of course, is why we keep sharp knives and scissors out of the way of small children, and place guards round fires when they are present. The things that attract them most are so often those they should not have.

What we often do not realize is that this is true of most of us. It is worth asking ourselves now and then if we really would be happy if we had all the things we think we want. We are fortunate indeed if we can pray sincerely and trustfully, " Give us bread sufficient for the day," or with the Greek writer, Menander, " Let not that happen which I wish, but that which is right."

JULY

FRIDAY—JULY 1.

GRANDMA was asking her seven-year-old grandson how he fared in his school sports.

"I ran for my team," replied Simon proudly, "and was the only one to come in last."

Better late than never!

SATURDAY—JULY 2.

IN her book *English Lakeland*, Doreen Wallace, herself a Cumbrian, deliberately omits information about climbing—that activity so popular with visitors to the Lake District—leaving writing about it to the experts.

Hills and fells, however, are a different thing, she says. "Anyone with a sound heart can walk uphill. And the rewards are so great. A little puffing and blowing is a small price to pay for all the kingdoms of the earth and the glory of them spread at one's feet; for the exhilaration of breathing rarefied air; for being literally on top of the world."

Well, maybe the time comes when most of us are beyond even that, but I love her phrase about "a little puffing and blowing" being a small price to pay. Not necessarily physically, but in terms of effort and determination, it is a bit of "puffing and blowing" that opens up to us most of life's joys—playing a musical instrument, appreciating a good book, mastering a hobby, understanding an exhibition of pictures or sculpture, learning about an ancient building. Isn't it worth a bit of "puffing and blowing" to share such riches?

SUNDAY—JULY 3.

OH that I had wings like a dove! for then would I fly away, and be at rest.

MONDAY—JULY 4.

HOW'S this for a loving husband?" asks Mary Cook of Warwick. "The other day I was trying my hand at making fudge—not very successfully. Seeing the gooey, runny stuff in the pan, and my disappointment, Hubby said, ' Never mind, love—we'll eat it, even if we have to DRINK it!'"

TUESDAY—JULY 5.

DO you know the story of the little girl in Kentucky, who was left motherless at the age of eight?

Her father was poor, and there were four children younger than herself; she tried heroically to care for them all and for the home. To do it, she had to be up very early in the morning and work till late at night. When she was 13 she fell very ill. One day a neighbour was sitting by her bedside when the girl said, " It isn't that I'm afraid to die, for I'm not. But I'm so ashamed."

" Ashamed of what?" asked the neighbour.

" You know how it's been with us since Mother died. I've been so busy, I've never done anything for Jesus, and when I get to Heaven and meet Him I shall be so ashamed. What can I tell Him?"

Taking the little calloused, work-scarred hands in her own, the neighbour gently answered, " I wouldn't tell Him anything, dear. Just show Him your hands."

THE FRIENDSHIP BOOK

D R ISAAC WATTS, the hymn writer, was a man of very small stature—something he was rather self-conscious about. He did not like to hear people describe him as " little Dr Watts."

I have sometimes wondered whether Watts was trying to come to terms with his lack of height when he wrote in one of his hymns:

Were I so tall to reach the pole
Or grasp the ocean in my span,
I must be measured by my soul—
The mind's the standard of the man.

Whatever Isaac Watts' feelings about his height, certainly it wasn't the measure of his life. He was a little man with a great heart and a great mind.

Some people seem to measure others merely in terms of material things. As someone once said, " When a man is alive, people ask, ' How much is he worth?' and when he is dead, they ask, ' How much has he left?' "

But as Isaac Watts said, it is the soul, the mind, which are the true measures of our worth.

T HE Lady of the House came in smiling the other evening. She had been chatting to Ada, whose husband recently retired. Ada told her that she had found him rearranging the contents of all her kitchen shelves.

" Didn't you try to stop him?" asked my wife. " Didn't you say something to him?"

" No," replied Ada calmly. " I just waited until he had finished—then I went down to the cellar and rearranged all his tools!"

H

FRIDAY—JULY 8.

ONE day by the roadside Dr Grey of Rossendale found a little dog with a broken leg.

He took it home, set the leg, and when the little dog was well, it began to run around the house. Then it disappeared. Doctor Grey never expected to see it again. But he was wrong! Next day there was a scratching at his door—and when he opened it, there was the little dog and with him was another dog who was lame.

I think there's a parable in this simple story of two dogs. When help has been received—isn't it natural to want someone else to be helped, too?

SATURDAY—JULY 9.

WHEN the Humber Bridge—the longest cable-suspension bridge in the world—was opened, one of the casualties was the Humber ferry which had been in operation for 178 years. Captain Charles King had been skipper of the *Farringford* for 15 years, and he confessed he does not know how many crossings he has made, " Ferry skippers would go mad counting crossings—so they don't."

Just before the new bridge opened he said in a newspaper interview, " When we come in for the last time, yes, I'll be sad, but life goes on. This is all nostalgia, but it had its place."

How right he was! The memory of much in the past can keep us grateful and keep us hopeful—and there can't be much wrong with that.

SUNDAY—JULY 10.

A PROPHET is not without honour, save in his own country, and in his own house.

THE FRIENDSHIP BOOK

MONDAY—JULY 11.

I WONDER how many parents become embarrassed when their baby starts to cry loudly in church?

I was in my usual place one Sunday morning when a loud wailing began. The little old lady sitting next to me whispered: " You know, I'm sure God likes to hear that baby crying more than all the moans and groans in the world."

Well said!

TUESDAY—JULY 12.

I HEARD a story once of a man who was given a wonderful prize by a magician. " Whatever you can run round in five minutes shall be yours," the magician told him.

The man spent many weeks running to improve his speed. His plan was to run around the most expensive houses in the neighbourhood and encircle a few shops and a bank as well.

At last he told the magician that he was now ready to claim his prize. He set off along the planned course racing as fast as he could. But before the five minutes were up and he could complete his circular course, he became exhausted and collapsed.

Friends, many of whom he had neglected during the time he was in training, found him lying in the road. They lifted him up, nursed him and cared for him until he had recovered his strength. He then wrote to the magician informing him that his running days were over and thanking him for what he had done. He told the magician he had gained something greater than wealth—the riches of friendship.

DON'T FORGET!

Won't someone take us for a walk?
We're feeling rather bored.
The world is full of sights and sounds
—So much to be explored;
And all the doggie books advise
We need a lot of exercise!

WEDNESDAY—JULY 13.

ALTHOUGH it is some years since I read Bunyan's *Pilgrim's Progress* in its entirety I often turn to it and re-read passages which have helped me in the past. One such favourite passage which I re-read if I am feeling a bit discouraged is one of the incidents in Interpreter's House. Christian is shown a fire burning in the grate. A man is constantly throwing water on it but the fire continues to burn.

The mystery is explained when Christian is taken to the next room where, through a hole behind the fireplace, another man is pouring oil, so keeping the fire burning.

There *are* circumstances which " damp our spirits ", people we call " wet blankets " or who, as we put it, " pour cold water " upon suggestions we make. But there is an antidote to all this in those three great qualities we call faith, hope and love. Learn to cultivate these and we can easily defeat the efforts of the " cold water pourers "!

THURSDAY—JULY 14.

A FEW weeks ago the Lady of the House and I browsed round an antique fair. Many of the things going for high prices were the sort of articles that we threw out years ago as useless. There were old books and postcards, old-fashioned household utensils, stone jam jars and glass bottles, to mention just a few of the items.

Isn't it the same with values? We are apt to throw some of them out, too, as old-fashioned although we know in out hearts that they are precious. Like all the old things at that antique fair they are very well worth keeping!

FRIDAY—JULY 15.

A YOUNG unknown Jew wrote these words on the wall of the Warsaw Ghetto:

I believe in the sun, even if it does not shine.
I believe in love, even if I do not feel it.
I believe in God, even if I do not see Him.

Written at a time when all seemed dark and hopeless, this passage of faith and trust is one of the most inspiring I know.

SATURDAY—JULY 16.

L ILLIAN GISH, the actress, retained her vitality and charm to a remarkable degree right into her eighties. In a television programme she insisted on the adjustment of the studio lighting so that her eyes could have full play, for, she explained, the eyes were one of the most important channels of personality. " So much depends," she said, " on the eyes."

Someone else once called them " beauty's jewels," and there is more to it than lighting, eye exercise or taking vitamin C. Eye beauty depends also on the attitude of mind. Gratitude lights up our eyes; so does wonder. When we delight in the beauty of a flower, or a child's smile, our eyes shine. As they do when we are interested and enthusiastic about anything. Most of all, love lights up the eyes—love of anything pure and good and beautiful. Our eyes need never be dull and lustreless, and as they shine they will bring joy and beauty to those around us, too.

SUNDAY—JULY 17.

B LESSED are all they that put their trust in him.

MONDAY—JULY 18.

WE were talking about sermons—memorable and otherwise! My friend Thomas admitted that he often had difficulty in remembering what the preacher had said, but one Christmas sermon on the subject of " Giving " he vowed he would never forget.

He recalled the preacher saying that when we received a present it gave us one thrill, but when we gave a present we had three thrills: the first, in actually choosing and buying the gift; the second in parcelling it up; and the third, a few days later, when we saw, or pictured, their happiness in receiving it.

How true it is that happiness lies more in giving than in receiving!

TUESDAY—JULY 19.

TURNING the tap for water is such a frequent and commonplace action for us that we take the ever-ready supply for granted and it is only in a drought or if the water is turned off for some reason that we fully appreciate it.

I sometimes look at the letters H and C on the taps and think it really is a bit of a miracle. We come in cold and wet and there waiting for us is what Rupert Brooke called " the benison of hot water "; or, hot and thirsty, we can take a cooling draught. It was not as easy for St. Francis to get water as it is for us, but he could say, " Praise be my Lord for our Sister Water, who is very serviceable unto us and humble and precious and clean."

It wouldn't do us any harm to think of some of this the next time we turn the tap!

OASIS

Even in busy cities
Corners you can find
Of peace and tranquil beauty
To soothe the jaded mind.

THE FRIENDSHIP BOOK

IN his book, *A Private House of Prayer*, Dr Leslie Weatherhead wrote: " The trend of Nature is towards completion and perfection. My cut finger *tends* to heal. The scarred earth *tends* to become reclothed in living green. The tops of my garden trees were lopped off. Soon, the highest boughs, which previously were horizontal, pointed towards the sky. There was a trend towards beauty."

This is an encouraging, creative thought—that there is a natural power at work in our bodies, minds and spirits which tends towards perfection and wholeness. Sometimes, unhappily, we hinder that trend, but we *can* help it if we will. Sleep, relaxation, prayer, meditation, music, scenes of beauty, congenial friendships are different, but effective, means of helping this healing power within us on its way.

WHEN Ernesto Halffter, a distinguished Spanish composer, was a young man he took one of his musical scores to his famous master, Manuel de Falla. Nervously, yet hopefully, he waited while the great composer studied it.

At length de Falla said, " This is good, Ernesto. If you believe it is the best you can do, there is nothing more to say. But if you think you can improve it, then it needs more work. Anything that can be improved is not finished."

What was true for those master musicians is also true in our humbler attainments. We miss a lot of satisfaction if we are content to say of anything, " It will do ", when it is less than the best that we can offer.

FRIDAY—JULY 22.

BISHOP WILFRID WESTALL, whilst the Suffragan Bishop of Crediton, was once visiting a remote parish church for a confirmation service. When he arrived he was met by the vicar and a helpful young man who volunteered to carry the Bishop's bag.

"Thank you," said the Bishop, and added, "You will find my kit in the boot of the car."

When he was robed and arrived at the altar, he found laid out, all cleaned, his jack, two spanners, a hammer and a wheel brace!

SATURDAY—JULY 23.

AFTER the last war many of our cities were left with ugly bomb sites. Nature soon took over and filled them with masses of lovely wild flowers.

In recent years this has become a deliberate policy in some places. In a fascinating book, *The Endless Village,* the author, W. G. Teagles, describes how, in the city of Birmingham, derelict ground, railway embankments, industrial wasteland, canal banks and similar places have become the habitat of plants and animals.

There is a lot of ugliness about us—not only physical and material but moral and spiritual, too, yet it is not beyond the power of most of us to do something to "reclaim" some of these sites. "Packets of seeds and good deeds" can do much to brighten the world.

SUNDAY—JULY 24.

GOD is our refuge and strength, a very present help in trouble.

THE FRIENDSHIP BOOK

DR STEPHEN WILLIAM HAWKING is one of Britain's leading scientists. The world acknowledges him as an authority on the astronomical phenomenon known as "black holes".

Quantum mechanics, thermo-dynamics, and general relativity are three distinct fields of physics which Dr Hawking has mastered. So remarkable is his ability to work out complicated mathematical equations mentally that one of his colleagues has likened it to Mozart composing an entire symphony in his head.

Yet this brilliant man has been confined to a wheelchair for years with an incurable disease which means he cannot write and at times can barely speak.

I am told that he never lets his physical problems get him down. All who meet him remark on his puckish sense of humour, his twinkling eyes, and an inner determination to let nothing — absolutely nothing — beat him.

If he is not a hero, then who is?

DURING the very last Gentlemen versus Players cricket match in 1962, batsman Peter Parfitt was caught out by the Rev. David Sheppard, now Bishop of Liverpool, who was then a member of the England team. Returning to the dressing-room, the batsman apologised to his captain, Freddie Trueman.

"That's all right, Peter,'" declared Freddie. "When the Reverend puts his two hands together, he stands a better chance than most of us!"

OFF WE GO

Life is full of new adventures,
*   Things to do and things to see*
In a world of many marvels,
*   But it's better, you'll agree,*
To explore this wonderland
Holding someone else's hand.

THE FRIENDSHIP BOOK

ALBERT was an ex-Serviceman who had been wounded in the war, and whose home had been struck by an enemy bomb. He had never been able to forgive the Germans.

Then one Sunday in church a member of the congregation had a heart attack. Albert went to him, put his coat under him, and kept him talking quietly until medical help arrived. The victim of the heart attack turned out to be a former German prisoner-of-war who had settled in Britain.

Albert felt rebuked for his long years of hatred. It all seemed so meaningless. " Suddenly," he said, " we were just two old men, hundreds of miles and several generations away from it all, sharing a coat and a conversation."

THERE can be few of us who have not at some time stood under the night sky recalling Jane Taylor's lines:

> *Twinkle, twinkle, little star,*
> *How I wonder what you are!*

But if tradition is to be believed, Jane wasn't standing out under the vast heavens when that inspiration came to her. She was peeping through the window of her house at Lavenham in Suffolk.

Sometimes when we are shut in through illness or age or infirmity it is worth remembering that when we have a window we have a view on to the world, on to the Universe! Good as it is to get out, we need never really feel " cribbed, cabined and confined " when a glance through the window can bring us at least something of the busy world without and the beauty of earth or sky.

FRIDAY—JULY 29.

A LITTLE girl in Sunday School was asked if she knew the story of Adam and Eve. She replied: "First God made Adam; then He looked at him and said: 'I think I can do better,' so then He created Eve!"

SATURDAY—JULY 30.

WHEN I was a boy, our local sweet shop was kept by an elderly couple who, at quiet times, used to take it in turns to serve in the shop. We used to peep inside to see who was serving, and if it was Mr B. we would go in for a pennyworth of our favourite slab toffee. But not if Mrs B. was serving! You see, the toffee had to be broken off the slab with a hammer and if a bit too much went into the bag Mrs B would keep chipping off bits till it was the exact weight!

With Mr B. it was different. Even if the scales went down with a bump, he would whip the bag off, twiddle it over to fasten the top and cheerfully toss it across to us.

Jesus talked about "good measure, pressed down and shaken together and running over." How much happier we should be, and how much happier we could make other people, if we were always on the look-out for the bit extra we could give or do.

SUNDAY—JULY 31.

THE Lord is my strength and my shield; my heart trusteth in him, and I am helped: therefore my heart greatly rejoiceth; and with my song will I praise him.

AUGUST

MONDAY—AUGUST 1.

DO you know this ancient but lovely Chinese proverb?

" You cannot prevent the birds of sadness from flying over your head, but you can prevent them building nests in your hair."

TUESDAY—AUGUST 2.

ALTHOUGH written more than 100 years ago, George Borrow's *Wild Wales* remains one of the most delightful travel books about that country which I have ever come across. Not only does it contain enchanting descriptions of the magnificent scenery and fascinating thumb-nail character sketches of the Welsh people, but it is packed, too, with examples of Borrow's shrewd philosophy of life.

On one occasion he had misunderstood directions given to him so that he arrived at the wrong inn. It proved to be a disappointing experience.

But George Borrow was not one to brood on adverse circumstances. " I looked at the bill," he said, " and whether moderate or immoderate, paid it with a smiling countenance . . . Reader, please to bear in mind that as all bills must be paid, it is much more comfortable to pay them with a smile that with a frown."

Life has its debts and duties, its disappointments and frustrations but if, like Borrow, we can learn to pay the bill with a smile, few things will get us down.

VISITORS to the Yorkshire industrial town of Halifax are usually intrigued by the 290-foot high Wainhouse Tower at the top of the town. Halifax people often speak of it as the Octagon tower, for this is its shape up to the first balcony. Then there is a 16-column colonnade, and the whole is crowned by a cupola.

Local legend has it that the tower was built in 1871 by John Wainhouse to overlook the garden of a neighbour who had built a high wall round it.

In fact, the tower was intended originally as a chimney for Wainhouse's dye-works in the valley below. Wainhouse, as other of his local buildings show, believed that if a man built he should build beautifully. Beauty as well as utility was his watchword.

It reminds me of the Biblical text, " strength and beauty are in his sanctuary." Perhaps we are all a little bit obsessed by utility in our modern way of life. Anything we can do to include beauty, too, will enrich the life of us all.

I SUPPOSE many fathers have amused their children by saying, " Press the button!" (i.e. Father's nose) and then pulling a funny face which had to be restored to normal again by pressing the chin.

But I wonder how many have had the experience of Rosemary's father, for, having pressed Daddy's nose and achieved an astonishing result, she walked across the room to her mother and said, " Look, Mummy! Let's leave him like that!"

AT EASE

> We all have our troubles and burdens to bear
>   That sometimes press hard on our backs;
> It is good to forget and to banish our care
>   Whenever there's time to relax.

FRIDAY—AUGUST 5.

IT takes a big man to acknowledge the fault when he has done something foolish. A friend who had been visiting Woburn, the famous home of the Dukes of Bedford, has been telling me how a former Duke tried to make sure one of his servants would not get the blame for something for which he was not responsible.

The Duke had planted a wood to mark the birth of his daughter. When the time came to thin it the Duke and his gardener had a strong difference of opinion. The gardener protested that if he did the job as the Duke wished, everyone would think he didn't know his trade.

" Do as I tell you," said the Duke, " and I'll look after your reputation."

The plantation was thinned according to the Duke's directions and when the job was done he put up a board for all to see. It read:

" This plantation was thinned by John, Duke of Bedford, contrary to the advice and opinion of his gardener."

SATURDAY—AUGUST 6.

EVERYBODY seems to have a different idea of what happiness means. The great German writer and philosopher Goëthe wrote " Who is the happiest of men? He who values the merits of others and in their pleasure takes joy *even though 'twere his own.*"

SUNDAY—AUGUST 7.

I WILL instruct thee and teach thee in the way which thou shalt go: I will guide thee with mine eye.

THE FRIENDSHIP BOOK

A FRIEND of ours who had always been a little apprehensive of flying told me how some words written by an aeronautical engineer gave him quite a new outlook. He was writing about efficiency in an engine and spoke about stresses and resistances—all a bit technical—but then he said, "The parts of an engine when working together in harmony actually seem to sing for joy."

It was those last words which helped our friend. Hitherto, the sound of the engine had frightened him. Now he listens for the joy in it. Let's listen for the glad sounds, and let's remember, too, that anything we can do to create harmony is also creating happiness.

THE Indian pacifist Mahatma Gandhi and the American Methodist Bishop Fred Fisher were great friends, and loved to tease each other.

One day the Bishop jokingly referred to the fact that two of Gandhi's front teeth were missing, and went on to suggest that Gandhi should visit his dentist in Calcutta. The Bishop offered to pay any necessary costs, and suggested that the replacement of the missing teeth would help both Gandhi's appearance and health.

Gandhi gently refused. He said: " Some years ago I renounced personal property and money; I began to live on the scale that the poorest of our people must live upon. I have kept my personal expenditure within 11 cents a day. One of our lowly brothers, whom I call sons of God and others call outcasts, could never afford your dentist. So I cannot accept, but I thank you deeply."

THESE days, some people seem to be getting rather cynical about the family—the institution which has been for so long the bulwark of our national life. I heard of a speaker at an open air meeting who declaimed: " Why can't all the nations live together like one big family?"

" That's the trouble," retorted a heckler. " They do!"

Thankfully, however, there are still many happy and harmonious families in our midst. I know of one where, before any big decision is made, say about a holiday, a new colour scheme for the dining room or alteration to the bathroom, a family conference is held. Even the baby in his high chair is brought into the circle!

That's just one way—and there are others open to us all—to make the family the centre of things again.

GALILEO, the pioneer Italian astronomer, is best remembered for his work based on the theory of Copernicus that the sun, rather than the earth, is the centre of our universe. He was also the first man to use a telescope.

One day someone asked him how he could reconcile the vastness of the universe with the idea of the care of God for every one of His creatures. His reply bears thinking about, especially as on first reading it doesn't even seem to be an answer to the question asked. He said: " The sun, which has all those planets revolving around it, is able to ripen the smallest bunch of grapes as though it had nothing else to do in the universe."

THE FRIENDSHIP BOOK

A MINISTER in British Columbia had a parish consisting largely of islands, and on one occasion was holding a service in the cabin of his small steamer on the British Columbian coast.

His congregation consisted mainly of loggers and miners. He had just opened his Bible when a cry came from the shore that a man had been desperately injured. Immediately the minister ordered a change of course and the whole party sped on their errand of mercy.

One of the loggers, a big, bronzed, bearded man, afterwards declared, "That was the best sermon I ever heard in my life!"

SIR HUMPHRY DAVY, inventor of the Safety Lamp for miners, believed in simple things.

As a boy he liked nothing better than to share his pleasures with other boys less fortunate than himself. They may not always have appreciated his methods for when quite young he used to enjoy reading aloud Bunyan's *Pilgrim's Progress* while seated in a cart with an audience of small boys who could not read.

In later years, he said: " Life is made up, not of great sacrifices or duties, but of little things, in which smiles and kindnesses and small obligations given habitually, are what win and preserve the hearts and secure comfort."

TRUST in the Lord and do good; so shalt thou dwell in the land, and verily thou shalt be fed.

MONDAY—AUGUST 15.

DR. NORMAN VINCENT PEALE tells us in one of his books of a voyage from the Mediterranean back home to America. The trip started in glorious weather and a calm sea, but in less than 24 hours a terrific storm raged. Afterwards they sailed into calm seas and sunshine again.

When he spoke to the captain about these sudden changes, the experienced seafarer told him, " I have always lived by the philosophy that if the sea is smooth, it will get rough; if it is rough, it will get smooth. But with a good ship you can always ride it out."

How true this is of life. No storms last for ever. With faith and hope and courage we can sail through them and emerge into the sunshine again.

TUESDAY—AUGUST 16.

AN Indian missionary has told of how, walking along a road one very dark night, he caught up with someone walking slowly and carrying a lantern.

" May I walk along with you?" asked the man with the lantern.

" Yes, certainly," said the missionary who, after a few moments, discovered that his companion was blind.

" I expect you wonder, " said the man, " why I carry a lantern when I am blind?" And, without waiting for an answer, he explained, " It is so that others may not stumble over me."

Being blind he could do little to help others but one thing he could do—he could make sure he did not hinder them.

THE FRIENDSHIP BOOK

GEOFFREY was a teenage student who wanted to do his bit towards improving relationships between different nationalities. He heard of a lonely old lady and called to ask if she would allow two immigrant boys to visit her home one evening. If she chatted to them it would assist them to become more fluent in the English language. Delighted to be of help, she immediately said yes.

The teenager then approached two of his immigrant friends and told them of a lonely old lady who needed a little company. He asked if they would visit her one evening each week for a chat. Eagerly they agreed.

Geoffrey had the right idea. The world is full of people who want to help others, but simply don't know how to begin.

THE Rev. Fridolin Ukur was on his way to Djakarta to give a lecture on the subject " Jesus Christ in Asian suffering and hope ". As he drove along, he passed a man lying by the roadside, but as he didn't want to be late for his lecture, he didn't stop to help. Many others also passed by.

Later that night, when the rickshaw-drivers swarmed into the city, they saw the man by the roadside and took pity on him. They lifted him into one of their vehicles and took him to hospital, leaving him there to be nursed back to health. Not only that, they left money to pay for special care.

This was in 1977, and ever since then the Rev. Fridolin Ukur has tried to make amends by retelling this moving story of the Indonesian Good Samaritans—and his own failing.

THE WANDERERS

*It's good to go exploring
When we are young and keen,*

*To feast our eyes on beauty
And keep its memory green.*

THE wedding service was charming, and the bride's father, a minister from Belfast, added what I'm told is an old Irish blessing:

May the road rise to meet you,
May the winds always be at your back,
May the sun shine warm upon your face,
The rains fall soft upon your fields,
And until we meet again—
May God hold you in the palm of His hand.

A lovely benediction, I thought, not only for the newly-weds, but also for all the guests, many of whom would probably not meet again for some time.

ON the shore at North Berwick is a large rock known locally as the Black Rock. One day, many years ago, a small boy (he later became a Judge in the High Court) got stuck half-way up. He thought he was about to go hurtling down to the beach below when over the edge of the rock came a long, thin arm. " Take hold of my hand," said a voice, " and when I say ' three,' jump!"

The boy seized the hand and was hauled to safety. There, on top, was another boy—Robert Louis Stevenson. " I owe everything worth having," the Judge wrote later, " to that lean, brown hand that came over the edge of the Black Rock long ago, and took charge of me."

It is not always possible to have the physical opportunity of holding out a rescuing hand to someone, but the " helping hand " can be a very real part of our daily life, and we may never know how much it can mean to someone.

SUNDAY—AUGUST 21.

BLESSED is that man that maketh the Lord his trust, and respecteth not the proud, nor such as turn aside to lies.

MONDAY—AUGUST 22.

LITTLE David came home from the new school he had been attending for just one week and reported proudly, " you can tell we're all getting more friendly now—we've started fighting!"

TUESDAY—AUGUST 23.

HAVE you ever heard of Samuel John Mills of Connecticut?

While he was ploughing, he sensed a call to preach the Gospel. Four years later when he entered college to prepare for the Christian ministry, he and five others with a concern for the salvation of the heathen met frequently in a grove of maples near the college campus for fellowship and prayer.

One day they were caught in a sudden thunderstorm, and sheltered against a nearby haystack. Ever afterwards, these gatherings were known as the Haystack Prayer Meetings. They developed into the American Baptists, who at first had no churches, but met and prayed around their haystacks.

Soon they initiated the U.S.A.'s first foreign missionary agency which began its work in February 1812.

From such humble beginnings came the inspiration for the work which still goes on all around the world telling others of the love of Jesus.

WEDNESDAY—AUGUST 24.

A GRANDFATHER was walking with his little grandson at the seaside on a very hot day when they met an elderly man whom the grandfather knew. Now the old man was not a very cheerful companion at the best of times, always full of complaints of one sort and another. On this occasion his mood was made even worse by the fact that, as he put it, he had had " a touch of the sun ".

The small boy had listened in silence to the old man's complaints, but as they moved on he whispered, " Grandpa, I hope you never suffer from a sunset!"

Well, he had mixed up " sunstroke " and " sunset ", but perhaps there was more truth in what he said than he realised. Some people *do* suffer from " sunsets "! We talk of people being " old before their time ", people who lose all their enthusiasms. If we remember Robert Browning's words: " Grow old along with me, The best is yet to be," we should be in no danger of suffering from a sunset!

THURSDAY—AUGUST 25.

A PART from being the author of the children's classic *The Water Babies* and the Elizabethan adventure novel *Westward Ho!*, the Rev Charles Kingsley had many other talents. One was the ability to give sound advice such as this:

" Have charity, have patience, have mercy. Never bring a human being, however silly, ignorant or weak—above all any little child—to shame and confusion of face . . . Never confound any human soul in the hour of its weakness."

CHERISHED

Some gardens are a few feet square
And some of spacious measure,
But all depend on loving care
To give a lifetime's pleasure.

THE FRIENDSHIP BOOK

FRIDAY—AUGUST 26.

THE story is told of Mahatma Gandhi that he was standing at the doorway of an open railway carriage as it moved slowly out of an Indian station, when one of his shoes slipped off and fell on to the track. Quickly he took off his other shoe and dropped that on to the track, too.

Seeing the puzzled look of a fellow passenger, Gandhi said, " A poor man may find a *pair* of shoes now; one wouldn't be much good to him."

I think it's one of the wonderful things about Gandhi that he rarely saw things in terms of how they affected him, but only in terms of how they affected others. Not a bad guide for life.

SATURDAY—AUGUST 27.

I HEARD recently of a man who attended a political conference wearing on the lapel of his coat a badge bearing the letters A.I.K. Someone asked him what it meant and he replied, " The letters stand for ' Am I Confused!' "

" But ' confused ' isn't spelled with a ' K '," said his questioner. " It is if you're as confused as I am!" was the retort.

I imagine many of us have a good deal of sympathy with him. It is not always easy to know what to believe or what direction to take.

To live a day at a time, to do what seems right at that particular time; this surely, is the way out of confusion, the path to peace.

SUNDAY—AUGUST 28.

FOR the Lord knoweth the way of the righteous: but the way of the ungodly shall perish.

THE FRIENDSHIP BOOK

A VISITOR to Washington once rang the chaplain attached to the White House and asked if the President was expected to attend church the following Sunday.

" I cannot promise that," replied the chaplain. " However, I have every expectation that God will be there, and that should be sufficient incentive for a reasonably good attendance."

JOHN RUSKIN, the famous art writer and critic, had on his desk a beautiful stone paperweight on which was carved the single word " Today ". It is said that he took this word as his own personal motto in preference to his traditional family Latin motto because he felt it was a more direct challenge to him as he contemplated it day by day.

There are some people whose motto seems to be " Yesterday "—they constantly live in the past; others take " Tomorrow " as their motto, indulging in day-dreams about the future.

Today well-lived
Makes every yesterday a dream of happiness,
And every tomorrow a vision of hope.

A MUM who was taking an Open University degree course was having trouble in persuading her little boy to go to school. Eventually, his 12-year-old sister did the trick. " Look, Ian," she demanded, " Do you want to grow up like Mummy, still going to school when you're 40?"

AROUND US

We only have to listen,
We only need to look,
To discover all the wonders
In history's open book.

SEPTEMBER

THURSDAY—SEPTEMBER 1.

MRS. ANNIE WELCH was ill on the day her daughter Vera was due to meet a rather special lady. The latter noticed that Vera was not at her happiest, and enquired what the trouble was. Vera told her that her mother was ill in hospital. The lady expressed her sympathy, and had a small gift sent round. Not only that but a few days later there was a call from Windsor Castle to ask after Mrs Welch.

That knack of going beyond the bounds of formal politeness has endeared Queen Elizabeth, the Queen Mother, to thousands, and not least to Vera Lynn and her mother.

FRIDAY—SEPTEMBER 2.

WHEN I am tempted to push a task aside saying , " I am too busy ", I try to make myself recall the words of Arnold J. Walker: " Everyone has the same amount of time. Whether he is a prince or a pauper, rich or poor, he has exactly the same amount of time as everyone else. The difference between success or failure lies in what you do with your time. Many people waste so much time explaining that they have not the time to do the things they want to do, that if they stopped talking and did some creative action they would be surprised at what they would accomplish."

Too many folk look on time as a very limited commodity, whereas, in fact it is an inexhaustible treasure.

K

SATURDAY—SEPTEMBER 3.

THE honeysuckle needs no voice to tell of its perfume. The burning stars do not shout to proclaim their glory. The grandest mountain stays ever silent. And this great old earth keeps turning.

The more profound the message, the less the need for words.

SUNDAY—SEPTEMBER 4.

FOR the word of the Lord is right; and all his works are done in truth.

MONDAY—SEPTEMBER 5.

A HOSPITAL chaplain told me a delightful story of an old lady whom he went to visit in hospital. As he approached her bed he noticed that with the index finger of one hand she was touching, one by one, the fingers of the other, with her eyes closed. When the chaplain spoke to her she opened her eyes and said, " Ah, minister, I was just saying my prayers—the prayers my grandmother taught me many years ago."

The chaplain looked puzzled, so she went on to explain, " I hold my hand like this, my thumb towards me. That reminds me to pray for those nearest to me. Then, there is my pointing finger, so I pray for those who point the way to others—teachers, leaders, parents. The next finger is the biggest so I pray for those in high places. After that comes the weakest finger—look, it won't stand up by itself, so I pray for the sick and the lonely and the afraid. And this little one—well, last of all I pray for myself."

Truly, a lesson in prayer for all of us.

THE FRIENDSHIP BOOK

LOTS of people like to be thought "tough". Years ago I copied down in one of my notebooks a paragraph from an unknown source: "Somehow we have the impression that to be real men we have to be tough and thick-skinned. But God never intended that we should have the hide of a rhinoceros. He has made us so sensitive that we may feel the caress of a breeze, the touch of a hand, the kiss of a child."

There is a place for both toughness and tenderness—tenderness towards others and their needs, but toughness with ourselves. In the words of Christina Rossetti:

> *God harden me against myself,*
> *This coward with pathetic voice*
> *Who craves for ease and rest and joys.*

WHAT is the secret of a long and healthy life? In order to find out, a few years ago a survey was carried out of over 500 people aged 95 and above in this country and America.

There was a good deal that might have been expected—sensible diet, reasonable exercise, the avoidance of over-weight. But apart from these physical factors, it was found that all these people had a similar mental attitude towards life. They shared a positive, optimistic outlook. They enjoyed living! This not only helped them to get more out of life as they went along, but it seemed actually to extend their span of life.

In those circumstances, no doubt they would all want to say with George Borrow, "Life is very sweet, brother; who would want to die?"

THE FRIENDSHIP BOOK

R OSITA FORBES was a woman who seemed to fear nothing. An explorer, she had exciting adventures in the Libyan Desert, the snow-bound passes of the Afghan-Russian frontier and other remote parts.

But she has some encouraging words for those of us who stay at home: " The scientist, the engineer, the steeplejack, the miner, the aviator all take the risks natural to their professions. Ordinary people in homes and offices might get a good deal of satisfaction by risking the new and the unexpected. Why stick to the same colours, the same routes, the same dishes, books, thoughts, words? Why not risk being original?"

We, too, can savour adventure!

I WAS with a group of friends when the conversation turned to the subject of our favourite food. The choice was wide-ranging—from herrings to haggis, from duckling to dumplings and indeed, to some quite exotic foreign dishes some of us had never heard of!

One of our company sat quietly in the corner saying nothing till he was addressed directly, " Come on, Angus, what about you?"

" My favourite food . . . ?" He smiled. " My favourite food is whatever my Jennie pleases to set before me!"

What an appreciative man! What a man for a wife to cook for! He reminded me of the saying in the book of Proverbs, " Better is a dinner of herbs where love is, than a stalled ox and hatred therewith."

THE FRIENDSHIP BOOK

SATURDAY—SEPTEMBER 10.

A L KORAN, the magician, once said " I love the things I am doing. I love going on to the stage . . . I love my audiences everywhere, the car I drive, my home, my family, my tropical fish . . . I love the mountains, museums, music, and flowers. The sky is never so blue, the birds never sing so sweetly, our friends are never so gracious, as when you are filled with love."

SUNDAY—SEPTEMBER 11.

O UR heart shall rejoice in him, because we have trusted in his holy name.

MONDAY—SEPTEMBER 12.

M ARIE WEBSTER of Gosforth, Newcastle upon Tyne, sent me these lovely lines:

My home's a place of warmth and rest,
With peace and solace there,
And Rover sits beside the fire,
Against the old armchair.
It is a place for building dreams,
And building strength and love
To meet the world of everyday
With guidance from about.

In springtime and in summer
There's fragrance everywhere,
With songbirds in the garden
Flitting through the air:
But when it's calm at sundown,
With gold upon the trees,
It's then I think the voice of God
Comes whisp'ring down the breeze.

THE FRIENDSHIP BOOK

THAT well-known organisation, the Women's Institute has branches in villages all over the country. Usually the name of the village precedes the title, Women's Institute. But there is at least one exception—"The Women's Institute of Ugley." Its members prefer it that way round!

The men of a hill-top village in Yorkshire are not so sensitive. They do not seem to mind their club being called the Idle Working Men's Club!

All good fun, of course. But how sensitive people are sometimes about things—about their size, their appearance, their age, the district they live in and so on. Some folk even change their names.

Yet how little such things really matter. Other people are usually far less conscious of them than we are ourselves.

Being our good, helpful, cheerful, best selves is the thing that really counts and that people remember about us.

AN eight-year-old pupil of Priorswood Primary School at Taunton won an essay competition with an outstanding account of the siege of Taunton in the English Civil War. His effort was adjudged the best out of several thousand entries.

Two years earlier, this prize-winning English essayist had not been able to speak a single word of English. Hung Dang arrived in this country as one of the refugee " Boat People " from Vietnam.

English isn't the easiest of languages to master but little Hung's achievement shows that where there's a will, there's certainly a way!

THE FRIENDSHIP BOOK

THURSDAY—SEPTEMBER 15.

I DON'T know who wrote these lines, but I think they are well worth passing on:

Don't look for the flaws as you go through life,
And even when you find them
It is wise and kind to be somewhat blind,
And look for the virtue behind them.
For the cloudiest night has a hint of light
Somewhere in its shadow hiding;
It is better by far to look for a star
Than the spots on the sun abiding.

FRIDAY—SEPTEMBER 16.

IT is now several years since Florence Whitehead of Manchester stumbled over a kerbstone and damaged her spine. Since then she has had many spells of being confined to bed, with the occasional visit to hospitals. She hasn't complained, though. She is able to write, knit, and even play the guitar.

Her special interest is painting, although before her accident she had never touched a paintbrush in her life. She started with a picture of a robin—a cheeky little picture which hangs on her wall at home. She progressed to 40 oil paintings in less than a year. One of her paintings won a prize—a restful picture entitled "Serenity"—an illustration of her own state of mind. All the other competitors were fully able-bodied, some of them had been lifelong painters, but Florence Whitehead, with an injured spine and not much previous experience, took one of the three prizes.

It shows I think, that it isn't what happens to us that matters most, it is how we react to what happens, and Mrs Whitehead's reaction to her crippling injury has been entirely positive.

SATURDAY—SEPTEMBER 17.

JIMMY, the little boy who lives down the road, stopped his bike and came over to where I was trimming the hedge.

" Mr Gay, can you tell me what every man thirsts after?" he asked solemnly. " Why,— ' knowledge ', Jimmy," I replied, thinking it was perhaps for a crossword puzzle.

" Ha! I got you that time—it's kippers!" and he cycled off quickly, grinning all over.

He's right, too!

SUNDAY—SEPTEMBER 18.

WHOSOEVER shall do the will of my Father which is in heaven, the same is my brother, and sister, and mother.

MONDAY—SEPTEMBER 19.

MRS MITCHELL made her very first plane trip recently. She had been worrying about it and as the plane soared into the air she looked down at the receding ground in terror.

Then a friendly young air hostess came along and pointed out of the window. " I think you'll feel much better if you look up," she said. Whereupon Mrs Mitchell lifted her head and saw the most glorious view of sunlit clouds against a silver-blue sky. " It was so wonderful," she said, " I forgot to be frightened." The rest of the flight was sheer pleasure.

I think we can all learn from Mrs Mitchell's story, even though our feet are firmly on the ground. How often we miss the beauty of creation because we are looking down instead of up!

THE FRIENDSHIP BOOK

AFTER retiring from her work at the Convent, Sister Marie lived happily in a little cottage at a holiday resort on the east coast.

In common with every other household, she received a Census form in 1981. This was the first time she had needed to fill one in, and she asked the local Methodist minister to help her complete it. She demurred, however, about recording her age.

"We've got to put in something," said the minister.

Sister Marie said: "Well, you know Mr and Mrs Hill across the road? I'm the same age as them."

So, very diplomatically, the minister completed the appropriate section of Sister Marie's form. Under "Age" he wrote: "As old as the Hills."

SOME time ago the Lady of the House and I visited a friend who has taken a new house on the outskirts of one of our big cities.

"You know, I love this house," he said, as we sat at the window with the traffic whizzing by. "Some people wonder why I chose a house here on the main road   but come through here."

He led us into a room at the back. Through the French windows we looked out on a vista of green fields, woodland, and the hills beyond.

He had two views—one of the busy world, the other of the peace of the countryside. Just like life, which contains seedtime and harvest, cold and heat, summer and winter, day and night.

Rest and activity are of life's very nature. Fortunate are we if we have both views.

THE FRIENDSHIP BOOK

LLOYD GEORGE used to tell the story of a doctor, greatly respected around Criccieth in Caernarvon, who, when he lay dying, was visited by the minister who asked him whether there was any last word or message he would like to give. There was a long pause as the old doctor painfully raised himself on his elbow. " No," he said,—and there was another pause—" except perhaps this. Through life I have always closed the gates behind me."

Not apparently very momentous last words—yet how significant in fact they are. To have performed life's simple courtesies, fulfilled its ordinary duties, done the things which would save other people trouble—this surely is to have lived a worthwhile life. Indeed, when I think about it, there could be worse epitaphs than, " He always shut the gates behind him."

I LIKE the story of the missionary new to his job who found that the workers in the fields on the mission estate carried their loads of stones and soil in baskets on their heads. Thinking to ease what seemed to him an unnecessary burden he made arrangements for each of them to be supplied with a wheelbarrow. Next time he saw them they were carrying the loaded wheelbarrows on their heads!

I suppose we have a right to laugh at that story only if we never misuse any of life's gifts ourselves—time, opportunities, food, freedom, humour. Do we always use them in the right and proper way?

THE FRIENDSHIP BOOK

I DON'T know what made me think of it because it happened many moons ago, but I'd like to share the story with you.

My friend Charles and I were visiting relatives of his in the old town of Frome in Somerset. As we left the train Charles promptly picked up my large suitcase as well as his own and began marching along the platform. I chased after him, of course, and insisted that there was no reason why I could not carry my own case. Charles just smiled and explained that two cases were easier than one because the weight was perfectly balanced.

Sometimes by helping others our own burden is eased.

COME unto me, all ye that labour and are heavy laden, and I will give you rest.

IN an interview on television, Sir Colin Davis, conductor of the Royal Opera, Covent Garden, was asked about the secret of successful conducting. He answered, " I think the real secret is that there must be love in it—love of the music, love of the people who are playing and of those for whom it is being played."

" There must be love in it ". Not just deep knowledge and skilful techniques, but love.

We may never excel in music in the way Colin Davis has done, but we can certainly make our own sort of music if we learn to love life and everything about it.

DREAMLAND

Some trees, a sward, a sunny glade,
A lazy, wandering stream,
Good friends for company and you have
The making of a dream.

A FRIEND of ours makes a practice of walking round his garden last thing at night just before going to bed. In summer or winter, whether it is light or dark, he finds here peace of mind.

One night, however, when he was feeling anxious and depressed, his beloved garden seemed to reflect his mood. The night was black. The trees were dark and shadowy. Then, as he glanced up he saw the top of a tree caught in the light of a street lamp. A patch of leaves seemed to be turned to pure gold! That gleam in the darkness sent him to bed with renewed hope. " It seemed like a miracle," he said.

I think, if we would look, there always *is* a gleam in the darkness.

L ORD MORLEY once said, " Try for yourself what you can read in half-an-hour. Then multiply the half-hour by 365 and consider what treasures you might have laid by at the end of the year; and what happiness, fortitude and wisdom they would have given you during all the days of your life."

We might well put that little exercise into practice with regard to reading, but it struck me how much more there is which, given say, only quarter of an hour, five minutes even, would multiply into an astonishing amount in the year—a period of prayer, of Bible reading, of writing up a diary, a few moments of complete relaxation, a phone call or a letter.

" Take care of the minutes and the years will take care of themselves."

THURSDAY—SEPTEMBER 29.

JIMMY, the small son of some young friends of ours, came home from school quite excited with a new bit of " arithmetic " he'd learned.

" What is four take away one, Mum?" he asked.

" Why, three, of course," replied Mother.

" I can show you that the answer is five," Jimmy said with a grin. He went into the kitchen and came back with a pair of scissors and a square sheet of paper.

" There are four corners on that paper, aren't there?" he asked.

" Yes," agreed Mother.

" Well watch!" Jimmy cut off one corner. " Now there are five corners left," he said triumphantly." " Four take away one is five!"

One up for Jimmy!

FRIDAY—SEPTEMBER 30.

THE Lady of the House and I were recently wandering round a textile museum and discovered that there was once a group of workers known as " perchers." These were people whose job it was to examine the finished cloth. Few pieces were absolutely perfect, and few so bad as to be rejected. With most it was difficult to decide if they should be passed or sent for repairs.

Isn't it the same with people? Few are downright saints or sinners. The words of E. W. Hoch are apt here:

There is so much good in the worst of us
And so much bad in the best of us,
That it hardly becomes any of us
To talk about the rest of us.

OCTOBER

SATURDAY—OCTOBER 1.

IT is many years now since Thomas Summers was a student at Cliff College when the much-loved Rev. Samuel Chadwick was the College Principal.

One day, during one of Mr Chadwick's lectures, Thomas found his attention wandering, and couldn't take any more notes. Next day he was summoned to the Principal's study. He entered in fear and trembling.

But Mr Chadwick's greeting put him at ease immediately: " Sit down, brother. Now tell me why you didn't take notes of my lecture yesterday morning."

Thomas tried to explain how at one point in the lecture he couldn't follow Mr Chadwick, that he had got hopelessly lost and couldn't pick up the threads of the subject again. Samuel Chadwick listened and then said, " I am very sorry, brother, I have always tried to avoid speaking beyond the ability of my students to understand, but it seems I don't always succeed. Such a thing will not happen again."

Principal Chadwick died in October 1932, but Thomas Summers has never forgotten the humility of a great man who knew how to command the love and respect of his students.

SUNDAY—OCTOBER 2.

O LORD my God, in thee do I put my trust: save me from all them that persecute me, and deliver me.

MONDAY—OCTOBER 3.

HENRY CROFT died on New Year's Day, 1930, after fifty years of philanthropic and charitable work on behalf of London hospitals. In ordinary life he was a humble road-sweeper and rat-catcher, but whenever he could he liked to dress up in suits encrusted with pearl buttons. He was acknowledged as the first Pearly King of London, and his memorial statue in St Pancras cemetery in Finsbury, depicts him resplendent in pearl-buttoned frock coat and top hat.

Every year on the first Sunday afternoon in October, the Pearly Kings and Queens congregate at St Martin-in-the-Fields for their annual Harvest Festival service. Their festival began after the Great War, and their gifts are sent to hospitals—a continuation of the work begun over 100 years ago by Henry Croft, whose sole purpose in attending numerous carnivals and festivals was to raise funds to help hospitals.

TUESDAY—OCTOBER 4.

WE have a friend called Daphne whom we see just once a year because of the distance between our homes. But, as the Lady of the House says, it's almost worth living so far apart because Daphne is such a superb letter writer.

Daphne collects quotes about friendship, and invariably ends her letter with one. Here's the latest which I'd like to share with you. It's by Hilaire Belloc:

From quiet homes and first beginning,
Out to the undiscovered ends,
There's nothing worth the wear of winning,
But laughter and the love of friends.

THE FRIENDSHIP BOOK

HENRY VISCARDI, a man without legs, wrote some lines from which I quote this moving passage:

> *I asked God for strength, that I might achieve;*
> *I was made weak, that I might learn humbly to obey.*
> *I asked for health, that I might do great things;*
> *I was given infirmity, that I might do better things.*
> *I asked for riches, that I might be happy;*
> *I was given poverty, that I might be wise.*
> *I asked for all things, that I might enjoy life;*
> *I was given life, that I might enjoy all things.*
> *I am, among all men, most richly blessed.*

PEOPLE who maintain their health and vigour long beyond the traditionally allotted span of three score years and ten seem to have a surprising variety of " secrets " for their longevity.

Some are vegetarians, others are meat eaters. Some are teetotallers while others enjoy " a wee dram " daily. Some take regular exercise, while one lively octogenarian told me, " I get all the exercise I need walking to the funerals of friends who have overdone their physical exercise!"

However, another old man explained it this way: " I think it is because I have never lost my enthusiasms."

It doesn't much matter what the enthusiasm is—books, flowers, music, friends, a charitable cause, church life, stamp-collecting, writing poetry—as long as it is something that completely engrosses us. This is the real elixir of life!

FRIDAY—OCTOBER 7.

FINE words butter no parsnips.

I came across this proverb in an old book the other day and I wonder whether you, like me, feel inclined to disagree with it. I think a sweet smile can turn a simple meal into a king's banquet, and loving words add flavour to the plainest fare.

SATURDAY—OCTOBER 8.

JOHN ADAMS of Chelmsford had been out of work nine months. He had applied for many jobs, but at the age of 48 no-one seemed to want to know him. Then he noticed another advert for a job he knew he could do. The only drawback was that it said: " under 45 preferred ". He applied, got an interview, gave his age as 44, and was told by the manager, Mr Benson, that he was just the man they were looking for.

When he got home, however, he seemed ill at ease. John's wife knew what the problem was—and told him he could not live with a lie on his conscience. Next morning he went back to see Mr Benson and confessed that he had lied about his age.

The manager raised his eyebrows, asked why he had come back to tell him, and John Adams told him what his wife had said. " That proves you are the man we're looking for," said Mr Benson. " The job is still yours if you want it."

Isn't honesty *always* more rewarding?

SUNDAY—OCTOBER 9.

HE that is not with me is against me; and he that gathereth not with me scattereth abroad.

THE FRIENDSHIP BOOK

HIGH in the mountains of northern Norway is the Helsesportsenter, a health sports centre where folk with many different handicaps can come together and learn to rise above their problems.

They come in wheelchairs—and learn to ride on horseback. Blind men come—and walk and ski for several miles. Those not able to hold down a regular job arc encouraged to feed and care for the horses—and this helps them to feel they are needed again. All are enabled to relish what they *can* do, rather than dwell on their handicaps.

This praiseworthy development is the brainchild of Erling Stordahl, who has also organised international ski-ing courses for the blind for twenty years, without a single accident!

" If you put your hand into the hand of God," says Stordahl, " there are fantastic possibilities." He should know. He embodies qualities of leadership, courage, honesty, and an indomitable spirit which has made him one of Norway's best-loved sons.

It is hard to believe that Stordahl has been blind himself for over 40 years.

MY friend Jim was telling me about his grandson, Alex, who has just had his fifth birthday. When asked how he was settling in at school, Alex replied that most lessons were fine—except sums! " I don't know why they make me do the horrid things," he said. " Out of the ten we did today I got eight right and only three wrong."

RENEWAL

*Trees men planted long ago
—They never fail to thrill;
In Spring and Summer, Autumn, too,
They set all hearts aglow,
Giving in wealth of leaf and fruit
Earth's oldest, newest show.*

THE FRIENDSHIP BOOK

J. B. PRIESTLEY once wrote in the introduction to a book called *The Beauty of Britain*: " We live on one of the most beautiful islands in the world. When beautiful islands are mentioned we think of Trinidad or Tahiti. These are fine, romantic places, but they are not really as exquisitely beautiful as our own Britain."

Somehow, " the distant scene " always seems more enchanting to us. Glamour seems to lie at a distance—dullness close at hand!

We are all a little like the girl in the story of " the house with the golden windows " who did not realise that the windows of her own house shone like gold in the evening sunlight just as did those of the house across the valley in the morning. Let's look for the beauty close at hand.

THURSDAY—OCTOBER 13.

KITE-FLYING has long been popular in Japan. I read somewhere that in the villages shop-keepers sometimes stand outside their shops flying kites while waiting for the next customer! One of the most interesting customs is that of the children at the end of the year. They write on a kite something about themselves they don't like, let the kite go up and up and then cut the string so that the kite flies away, taking with it the fault they have named!

There are worse ways of marking the end of the year than by doing a bit of self-examination and really and determinedly " letting go " some of the things we know spoil our lives—the worries, resentments and jealousies.

" Let's go and fly a kite!"

FRIDAY—OCTOBER 14.

THERE is an old Arabian riddle which goes, " Who is richer, the man with a million dollars, or the one with seven daughters?" The answer is, " The man with seven daughters for he has enough and he knows it!"

Material possessions have a necessary and important part to play in our lives, but they never really satisfy.

There are people who, even as their circumstances improve, seem to go through life saying, " If only I had another fiver a week!"

As the Bible tells us, " a man's life consisteth not in the abundance of things which he possesseth."

SATURDAY—OCTOBER 15.

IN his novel " The Price of Love " Arnold Bennett has a description of Mrs Maldon's maid washing up. He writes: " Here was Rachel converting the horrid process into a dignified and impressive ritual. She made it as fine as fine needlework—so exact, so dainty, so proud were the motions of her fingers and her forearms. Obviously washing up was an art, and the delicate operation could not be scamped or hurried."

An exaggeration, perhaps? Yet what a difference it can make when we give that sort of care to simple, humble, perhaps uncongenial tasks. The commonplace *can* be transformed for us into something satisfying and rewarding.

SUNDAY—OCTOBER 16.

FOLLOW me, and I will make you fishers of men.

THE FRIENDSHIP BOOK

I SUPPOSE there are few subjects about which there is such a wealth of quotations, or so many pieces of advice given as that of happiness, but I came across a definition new to me the other day when I was browsing through a bound volume, some 50 years old, of a magazine some readers will remember, *Great Thoughts*.

It said, " Happiness is like manna. It is to be gathered and enjoyed every day; it will not keep; it cannot be accumulated; nor need we go out of ourselves or into remote places to gather it, since it is rained down from heaven at our doors, or rather within them."

Don't let us neglect to gather our ration of happiness today!

I CAME across these thought-provoking lines in a church magazine some years ago:

Are you an active member, the kind that would be missed?

Or are you just contented that your name is on the list?

Do you attend the meetings and mingle with the flock?

Or stay at home in comfort to criticise and knock?

Do you take an active part to help the work along?

Or are you merely satisfied just simply to belong?

Think it over, Members, you know right from wrong—

Are you an active member or do you just belong?

THE FRIENDSHIP BOOK

FOUR-YEAR-OLD Philip was very interested in the new little boy who had come to live with foster parents just down the road. Jason was six months younger than Philip, but hadn't had a very happy life so far. In fact he had very little to call his own—no toys at all. Philip's parents asked him if he would like to give anything to Jason.

Philip thought for a moment, and then surprised them by saying, " He can have my crane "—it was his much-loved and favourite present from the previous Christmas.

Jason is now a much happier little boy. He has settled down well in his new home with his new parents, and enjoys playing with his new friends and his new toys—particularly that lovely crane.

Bless you, Philip!

THERE are strange ways of earning a living. I heard recently of an American woman, widowed young, and with no occupational qualifications, who was faced with the necessity of supporting herself. She put an advertisement in a local newspaper saying that she was willing to listen to anybody talking to her about anything for two dollars an hour. The idea was an instant success and within two years she had a staff of 50 doing nothing but listen to people talking to them.

Hearing that story made me more determined than ever to be ready to listen. If there are people so lonely that they are willing to pay for someone to talk to there is surely an opportunity here for all of us to offer freely a little sympathetic listening. It is so easy—and can mean so much.

THE FRIENDSHIP BOOK

WHEN Winifred Holtby, the Yorkshire novelist, died at the early age of 37, she was mourned all over the world. Not only had she been a novelist and journalist, but a fearless campaigner for minorities. Some of this campaigning was in South Africa where she tried to interpret the white population to the coloured and vice versa. She was not only campaigning for human justice, but for an extension of education.

Her South African Memorial in Johannesburg is the Winifred Holtby Memorial Library.

In the countryside churchyard of Rudstone, near Bridlington, her gravestone carries the inscription:-

> God give me work
> Till my life shall end,
> And life
> Till my work is done.

NOT long ago I met Jill who recently became a widow. As we were talking she said something which stuck in my mind and which I've often thought about since. It was, " What a good thing time does not stand still."

Yes, time rolls on and as surely as winter turns to spring so hurts give way to healing and doubts can lead to faith.

CAST thy burden upon the Lord, and he shall sustain thee: he shall never suffer the righteous to be moved.

MONDAY—OCTOBER 24.

PUTTING our clocks forward and backward an hour in the spring and autumn has become a part of our life we take for granted

William Willett, the originator of the idea, had to campaign many years in face of much opposition and ridicule, and indeed, died shortly before his plans were put into practice.

I like particularly the circumstances in which the idea came to him. He used to rise early to go riding, and it was one bright summer morning in 1907 that he noticed the blinds still drawn in most of the houses he passed and thought, what a waste of daylight! From this simple thought sprang his revolutionary idea.

Willett wanted others to share his delight in the morning. Well may we sing with Eleanor Farjeon,

Mine is the sunlight,
Mine is the morning!

TUESDAY—OCTOBER 25.

ALAN BRECK in Robert Louis Stevenson's novel, *Kidnapped*, says, at one point, " I have a grand memory for forgetting." I suppose he meant he had what we would call " a bad memory "—which can be an embarrassment at times, as in the case of the man who greeted someone he had met only once before with the words, " Good morning Mr Pickles," only to be met with the cold retort, " The name is Onions!"

All the same, there is a place in life for forgetting, as well as for remembering. Resentments and slights, past misfortunes or handicaps, mistakes which cannot be remedied — how much better that all these should be forgotten.

THE FRIENDSHIP BOOK

A N elderly minister retiring from his pastorate received, as parting gifts from his congregation, a handsome cheque, a clock and a specially inscribed Bible.

Some time later an elder of the church was visiting the minister and his wife in their new home and discovered the Bible lying on the table. He opened it casually to refresh his memory of the inscription and found that the minister had added at the bottom, " The cheque has gone, the clock is going, but the Word of the Lord abideth for ever."

S HE has a soft and woolly lamb,
She has a teddy-bear,
She has a doll who walks and talks,
With golden, curling hair;
But turns away from all of these,
And loves to make a din—
Drumming with a wooden spoon
On an old and battered tin!

S OME time ago I cut out these words by an anonymous writer: " If you see anything worthy of praise, speak of it. Even if you cannot do a worthy deed yourself, commend one who does. Praise is a power for good: both man and God prize it. The best worker, if his fellows fail to praise, fails doing as well as he can."

Sometimes, in our fear of flattery, we are too stinting in our praise. A little appreciation and encouragement can go such a long way.

SATURDAY—OCTOBER 29.

THE traveller Ulric Nisbet wrote: " Once upon a time I discovered the most delightful little village in the world, one above all others in beauty—a village of eternal peace and sunshine far distant from the path of man. Does it sound a little too good to be true, too perfect? . . . Well, it was not perfect. There were mosquitos! How often do they shatter our most romantic dreams. But I can afford to forget them, and I will. I am content to remember my village and to have given it my heart."

If only we could look at everything like Ulric Nisbet, who forgot the mosquitos and remembered the beauty.

SUNDAY—OCTOBER 30.

ASK, and it shall be given you; seek, and ye shall find; knock, and it shall be opened unto you.

MONDAY—OCTOBER 31.

A MISSIONARY has told how the yellow-robed Buddhist monks in Burma walk through the streets with their wooden bowls into which people place their gifts of food. If, however, the monks are displeased with the people for wrong behaviour of some kind they walk with their bowls turned upside down. The people's punishment is to be deprived of the privilege of giving!

We sometimes forget the Biblical saying, " It is more blessed to give than to receive " and it is easy to think of giving as being simply a duty and not a delight. Life's real happiness comes not so much from getting and having, as from giving and sharing.

NOVEMBER

THE Lady of the House was anxious that I should begin an overdue " face-lift " to our hall.

" It's no use stripping off the old paper today because I won't be able to start re-papering," I said. " I'll do it when I have more time."

That evening I read that Harriet Beecher Stowe wrote *Uncle Tom's Cabin* in odd moments between cooking meals and looking after her six children. Her biographer commented: " Had she waited until she had more time, that best-seller would probably never have been written."

I got the message! Next morning I began working in the hall.

CAN you create a vegetable plot or a flower garden from a small patch of bare earth? Do you paint, or knit, or write poetry? If so, you are fortunate indeed because, according to a doctor friend, creative people are less likely than most to suffer from deep depression.

I'm no expert on the human psyche, so I'll not agree or disagree with him. But this I do know — time spent making things is never wasted. And don't lose heart because the thing you are making is not a lot of use. A pebble is of little use; the same may be said of a snowdrop in winter. But they each have a purpose in the scheme of things.

Isn't it rather wonderful to think that we can all contribute, however humbly, to the beautiful things of this world?

THE FRIENDSHIP BOOK

OUTSIDE Derby Royal Infirmary is a statue of Florence Nightingale—an appropriate site, for she was instrumental in the hospital's foundation. Strangers to the city often ask about the carving of an owl at the foot of the statue, which at first sight would seem to have little to do with her nursing career.

But the story goes that as she was setting out for the Crimea, she came across a group of boys who were tormenting and ill-treating an owl. Although, she was in a hurry, she rescued the bird, and its presence on her statue is a reminder to us that her career sprang from compassion for " all creatures great and small."

She had always time to minister to the small need as well as the great. That *is* compassion.

HELEN KELLER once wrote: " The hands of those I meet are eloquent to me. I have met people so empty of joy that when I clasped their frosty fingertips it seemed as if I were shaking hands with a north-east storm. Others there are whose hands have sunbeams in them."

How eloquent a handshake can be! It can express welcome, encouragement, sympathy, agreement and much besides. Those who have studied the history of our human customs think that the origin of the hand-shake may have been in the holding out of the hand on meeting to show that it held no weapon, and that one came in peace.

The simple act of a friendly handshake can often say more than words. We are never speechless if we can shake hands.

THE FRIENDSHIP BOOK

FOR months he had been her devoted admirer. Now, at long last, he had mustered sufficient courage to ask her the most momentous question of all.

So he began: " There are quite a lot of advantages in being a bachelor, but there comes a time when one longs for the companionship of another being—a being who will regard one as perfect, as an idol; whom one can treat as one's absolute property; who will be kind and faithful when times are hard; who will share one's joys and sorrows . . ."

To his delight he saw a sympathetic gleam in her eyes. Then she nodded in agreement. " So you're thinking of buying a dog?" she said. " I think it's a fine idea. Do let me help you choose one!"

WHEN thou doest alms, let not thy left hand know what thy right hand doeth.

KEITH CASTLE underwent a heart transplant operation which was completely successful. Two years later he was asked how he regarded the future.

" Why, with great hope, of course," he replied. " I mean—look at the pansies in my garden, for instance. From those there will be seeds for next year's flowers and then, from them, seeds for flowers the year after that."

The right philosophy!

THE FRIENDSHIP BOOK

A BANKING magazine may not be a source to which we would automatically look for inspirational thoughts, but a friend found the following in *The Royal Bank of Canada Monthly Letter*: " If someone asks, ' Are you happy?' do not look into your stock of worldly goods, or into your pay envelope, or into your fame, but into your work. A man is made happier by *doing* things rather than by having delectable things wrapped in cellophane and laid on his knee."

However humble our calling may be, there is a satisfaction in work well done which can be equalled by few other things. I have often found great help in a prayer of Robert Louis Stevenson:

" O God, help us to perform our duties with laughter and kind faces; and let cheerfulness abound with industry. Give us to go blithely on our business all this day, and bring us to our resting beds weary and content and undishonoured; for Jesus Christ's sake."

S USIE, a London girl, went to visit her mother who had moved to a quiet country village. She was amazed by the unhurried pace of life. One day she ran to catch the bus, thinking the driver wouldn't wait. As she entered, out of breath, the driver said, " Take your time, luv, there's plenty of it. There's tomorrow not touched yet."

Of course, for most of us life has its dead-lines to be met, its appointments to be kept and so on, yet it might help to take a bit of the fuss and fret from our lives if we reminded ourselves now and again that " There's tomorrow not touched yet."

HARVEST FESTIVAL

When fruit has ripened on the tree
And grain is gathered from the field,
We place our offerings in the church
In thanks for one more season's yield.

M

THURSDAY—NOVEMBER 10.

THE late William Barclay, well-known preacher and author, says in one of his books that one day he had to write three letters—two of them letters of complaint. One was to the police about a traffic problem, one to the local postmaster about a postal difficulty and the last to the Inland Revenue with his tax form. He had delayed writing the letters because he wondered if he would be wasting his time.

Much to his surprise the police replied immediately thanking him for the complaint, and the matter was later put right. The postmaster said, " Thank you for writing " and put an end to his troubles, and the Tax Office told him to claim more!

Dr Barclay was pleased that he had written the letters and that his complaints had been dealt with so courteously and so quickly. He said that he had learned once more that when service is given with a smile, a glow spreads over life that makes everything we do doubly worthwhile.

FRIDAY—NOVEMBER 11.

JOYCE GRENFELL, the entertainer, was a person who, in private life as well as on the stage, simply bubbled over with the joy of living. One of her friends said of her, " She was so outgoing. When she opened the door to you, she didn't step backward—she stepped forward to greet you."

How much more friendly a place the world would be if we all tried to cultivate this attitude towards others! " Stepping forward " shows an eagerness to meet, to communicate, to welcome.

THE FRIENDSHIP BOOK

A SALESMAN whose work took him to every part of the country was once asked which he considered the most beautiful stretch of road in England. His answer was not, as might have been expected, some Devonshire lane, or a road in the Yorkshire Dales or the Lake District.

"For me," he said, "the most beautiful stretch of road in England is the last three miles into Middlesborough on a foggy November Friday night when I'm nearly home!"

Yes, indeed, "Be it ever so humble, there's no place like home."

Someone once wrote: "There is no house like yours. Windsor Castle is more lordly perhaps, but you cannot honestly say it is yours. A gorgeous place is Chatsworth, but you do not carry the key in your pocket. Your house is different from all the other houses in the world in one respect at least—it is *yours,* and when you are indoors you are at home."

THE foxes have holes, and the birds of the air have nests; but the Son of man hath not where to lay his head.

A NEIGHBOUR was telling the Lady of the House about a wedding she had attended. It was just lovely, she said and though, of course, the bride was the centre of attention, everybody was captivated by a very tiny bridesmaid who was, she said, "carrying a bunch of Friesians"!

THE FRIENDSHIP BOOK

THE world sets great store by what it calls wealth, but I wonder if we really understand what wealth is. That great nonconformist preacher of a former generation, Dr J.H Jowett, once said, " The real measure of our wealth is how much we should be worth if we lost all our money."

Think about it.

THE proprietor of a village store had a board in the window on which he displayed cards advertising things people wanted to buy or sell. One day in a magazine he came across a humorous cartoon about a village store and he pinned it to the centre of his board, outlined the cartoon in red and labelled it " This Week's Smile ". A day or two later a customer brought another, even funnier cartoon, also about shop-keepers, and next week it appeared in the central spot on the board.

Soon the idea caught on and the shopkeeper was inundated with cartoons and jokes, not always about shops but often on food and kindred subjects, village life and characters. Indeed, so great was the stock of material that " This Week's Smile " soon had to become " Today's Smile "! Nobody passed the shop without a glance in the window, and often they called in to leave their " smile " for future use.

When the local bobby saw the people round the window he jokingly told the shopkeeper that he would run him in for obstruction! But he knew that it would be more than his life was worth! Few things brought greater happiness to that little village than " Today's Smile ".

HANDEL'S "Messiah" makes a perennial appeal to music lovers but its impact is more than simply musical. When it was first performed in Dublin in 1742 it received a wonderful reception. A contemporary report said, " The audience was exceedingly struck and affected by the music in general but when the chorus struck up ' For the Lord God Omnipotent ' in the Alleluia they were so transported that they all, together with the King (George II) who happened to be present, started up and remained standing until the chorus was ended." It is a custom which has persisted to this present day.

Sometimes I think we are a bit squeamish about expressing our feelings, but simple physical actions can often show a good deal—standing at attention, waving flags, kneeling or bowing our heads in prayer, even a handshake. I know a church where, just as the service begins, each member of the congregation shakes hands with someone behind, or in front or across the aisle. Often our heart tells us to do something, but our mind stops us. It's a pity, for the heart is almost always right!

FRIDAY—NOVEMBER 18.

THOSE of you who love reading and have tried to build up your own collection of books, however small, will want to say " Amen " to Elbert Hubbard's words: " Books, like friends, should be few and well-chosen. Like friends, too, we should return to them again and again—for like true friends, they never fail us, never cease to instruct us, never cloy."

THE FRIENDSHIP BOOK

A FRIEND of ours who collects epitaphs says that one of his favourites, because it records character rather than achievements, is that on General Gordon's tomb in St Paul's Cathedral. It reads:

CHARLES GEORGE GORDON

Who at all times and everywhere gave his strength to the weak, his substance to the poor, his sympathy to the suffering and his heart to God. Who could wish for a better epitaph?

SEEK ye first the kingdom of God and his righteousness; and all these things shall be added unto you.

LISTENING one evening to a programme of hymn-singing on television I was reminded of some words written long ago by the Rev. H. V. Elliott, brother of the hymn-writer, Charlotte Elliott. He wrote, " In the course of a long ministry I hope I have been permitted to see some fruit of my labours; but I feel more has been done by this hymn of my sister's."

The hymn he referred to was, " Just as I am without one plea." But similar tributes could surely be paid to many another hymn and hymn writer. I know sometimes it is said that people just get carried away by a tune and don't pay any attention to the words they are singing. That *can* happen, of course, but I believe many of us can find real inspiration through hymns.

THE FRIENDSHIP BOOK

FOR many years Dr Harry Emerson Fosdick was minister of the famous Riverside Presbyterian Church in New York. His sermons and books must have brought inspiration to thousands, but a friend of mine tells me that it was little more than a single sentence of Dr Fosdick's which influenced him beyond anything else he can remember.

This was it: " Choose life! So many only choose existence. Existence is the raw material from which to fashion life."

AN old farmer friend was talking about a neighbour who was always grumbling about the weather. " He would like to have it raining on one of his fields and not on the one next to it!"

I suppose we all tend a bit towards wanting the weather to suit our own purposes. Don Lewis has written, " Sentimentalists pray for snow at Christmas, farmers for sunshine in July to ripen the harvest; gardeners and arthritics dread the frost, and mothers curse wet Saturdays. Thus, for good reasons or not, throughout generations of time, mankind has wished for control over the weather."

But in the last resort, we have to come to terms with it—and with many other circumstances of our lives over which we have no control. The writer of the book of Ecclesiastes shows valuable realism when he says, " He that observeth the wind shall not sow, and he that regardeth the clouds shall not reap." If we learn to do the best we can, whatever our circumstances, we will not have much cause for complaint.

THURSDAY—NOVEMBER 24.

IN his book *Memory Hold the Door,* John Buchan tells the story of a friend of his who visited some soldiers who'd returned wounded from Mesopotamia during the First World War. He asked one of them, a Scot, where he had received his wounds, and got the reply, " Twa miles on the Rothiemurchus side of Baghdad!"

To him, home was the point from which he measured all else, the centre of the universe. It may seem a narrow view to some, but life does need some point of security for us in our troubled world, our mysterious Universe. We may find it in different ways—through our home, as the Scottish soldier did; in our church; in our work; in our friends; in some consuming interest of our lives. The point is that it is something familiar and loved which becomes our centre round which everything else falls into place.

FRIDAY—NOVEMBER 25.

I HEARD recently about an old custom called the Grovely Forest Rights Ceremony in which bonneted ladies carrying bundles of wood dance on Salisbury Cathedral Green. It is part of a ritual by which the people of Wishford Manor renew their right to collect wood from the forest—" all kinde of deade snappinge woode, boughes and stickes," as the ancient document has it.

It all sounds a bit quaint, but what a lot of " ancient rights " we all can enjoy if only we will claim them—our freedoms of speech and worship, our friendships, our heritage in art, music and literature, the beauties of the countryside. Perhaps we *should* dance—for joy at all our limitless rights!

THE FRIENDSHIP BOOK

WHEN Robert Louis Stevenson was a small boy in Edinburgh he was often unwell and had to stay in his room. One winter evening as night fell, his nurse found him with his nose pressed to the window pane.

"Come away, Master Robert," she said. "You'll catch your death of cold."

"But, nurse," said Robert, "Come and look! There is something wonderful happening out here. There is a man going down the street making holes in the dark!"

I imagine it is a long time since any of us saw an old-fashioned lamp-lighter with his long pole. But what a lovely way of putting it—making holes in the dark!

And we can still do it, of course, for other people in the darkness of sorrow or need. A smile, the grip of a hand, a word of sympathy or encouragement—there are plenty of ways of being lamp-lighters!

MAN shall not live by bread alone, but by every word that proceedeth out of the mouth of God.

I HEARD the other day of a little Australian boy who was on holiday in Britain. When asked what he thought of the country, he pondered for a minute or two, then said, "Well, the language is different—but the laughing's just the same!"

Yes, he learned a fact of life—laughter's the same the world over.

TUESDAY—NOVEMBER 29.

I OFTEN dip into John Wesley's *Journal* and I never open the book without lighting on some gem of truth.

He tells in one place how he stayed with a man of undoubted piety, but whose life was marred by self-pity. His complaint to Wesley was almost unbelievable. As smoke puffed into the room from his fireplace he whined, " Ah, Mr Wesley, every man has his cross to bear and this is mine—a smoking chimney!"

Lucky man if he had nothing worse to complain of! Yet, perhaps the story does make us look at our own grumbles a little more closely so that we may be on our guard against magnifying our troubles out of all proportion when we ought to be counting our blessings.

WEDNESDAY—NOVEMBER 30.

I N a little northern fishing port, fish was offered for sale each morning on the quay-side, fresh from the sea. One night there had been a terrible storm but some fish was still landed for sale.

One customer examined what was displayed and then asked, " How much are haddocks this morning?"

Swiftly came the reply, " Haddocks are men's lives this morning!"

This is something we sometimes forget—fish from the sea, coal from the mines, food from across the ocean—all this is brought to us only at a cost. We ask the *price* of things, but this is often very different from the *cost*. How much more appreciative we would be if we contemplated the true cost of so much that we take for granted.

DECEMBER

THURSDAY—DECEMBER 1.

WHEN Sue Brown was elected the first-ever woman cox for Oxford in the Boat Race, she and her crew received all the attention from the media and Cambridge were almost completely neglected.

When the Cambridge cox was asked about his reactions to all this he said, " Well, the cox is usually neglected by the media so I suppose it's a good thing for coxing generally that all this publicity has brought the job into the limelight. I don't feel jealous—I suppose I just bask, in a way, in the reflected glory!"

Next time I'm tempted to any feelings of jealousy I will try to remember that anonymous cox.

FRIDAY—DECEMBER 2.

IN the museum at Fort William is a square piece of wood covered with what seems to be meaningless blurrs of paint. But when a polished steel cylinder is placed upright on the board a picture of Bonnie Prince Charlie is reflected on its surface! The board was a secret portrait of the Prince devised by his followers when it was forbidden to possess any likeness of the young Pretender.

All of which is a parable because often our lives seem to be made up of so many scattered, mysterious and sometimes even unpleasant features; yet, if we have faith and hope we can see a pattern and a purpose taking shape.

THE FRIENDSHIP BOOK

A FRIEND went to see a fortune-teller at a local fair. She was told her future seemed bright, although there were also some dark clouds on the horizon. Those dark clouds worried her and she came out feeling a little down. Then, as she made her way home she noticed a poster which read, " Worry never robs tomorrow of its sorrow, it only robs today of its strength."

My friend hasn't been back to the palmist. Nowadays she tries to let tomorrow take care of itself.

SUNDAY—DECEMBER 4.

A GOOD tree cannot bring forth evil fruit, neither can a corrupt tree bring forth good fruit.

MONDAY—DECEMBER 5.

I LOVE looking through old photograph albums. They give so much pleasure with their reminders of old friends, holidays and happy occasions.

Sometimes, sadly, old photograph albums find their way into second-hand shops. In one old album I found this verse written out:

Just as the summer bee will stray
Where rich bloom fills the woodland dells,
Bearing the luscious drops away
That help to store its golden cells;
So do we gather in this book
The great, the good, the kind, the dear,
And bless the pages while we look
On memory's honey gathered here.

NATIVITY

On a stable bare the stars shone down,
  Long centuries ago,
And still the wondrous tale we tell
  As ages come and go:
A tale that's plain to childlike eyes,
  Yet all we need to know.

PETER USTINOV has had a remarkably successful and varied career as actor, dramatist, director and raconteur. In a television programme the audience were given the opportunity to ask him questions about his work.

One question was, " Looking back over your career, are there pieces of work which you have accepted and then wished that you hadn't, or those which you refused and then wished later that you had accepted?"

" What's the point of having regrets?" asked Ustinov. " I have made mistakes—we all do. But no—once a decision has been made, there it is. It is no good having regrets."

The right spirit.

HOW do you greet a new day? I love the sentence in Bunyan's *Pilgrim's Progress,* " Christian slept till the break of day, then he awoke and sang."

If we are honest with ourselves we shall probably have to admit that the first waking sound we make is probably a yawn or a sigh.

It might not be a bad idea to do as Bunyan's pilgrim and sing a verse or two of a morning hymn, such as " Morning has broken ", " New every morning is the love " or " Awake my soul and with the sun ".

If we didn't want to disturb the rest of the household, we could always hum one of these quietly to ourselves. After all, the start of a new day is something rather special and well worth celebrating!

THE FRIENDSHIP BOOK

AMONG some of the most interesting programmes on television are those which show musicians and orchestras in the process of preparing and rehearsing for a performance.

Bernard Keeffe, the conductor, was rehearsing an orchestra of young people in one of these programmes and was explaining to the audience some of the difficulties involved. He pointed out that the young musicians needed powers of accurate music reading and technical control of their individual instruments. " One of the most important things," he said, " is that, as well as playing themselves, they must learn to listen to the other parts of the orchestra."

This is probably something which most of us have never really thought about, yet clearly the whole performance could be chaotic unless they listened to each other in this way.

Life itself is sometimes chaotic for the same reason—when we listen only to ourselves. Max Erhmann once wrote, " . . . listen to others, even the dull and ignorant; they, too, have their story."

If we are interested in people—genuinely interested in them—we can never be bored.

OPEN the book of memories
Whenever you feel sad,
And take a look at happiness,
The good times that you've had.
Be cheered by those small loving acts,
The unexpected treat,
The word of praise, forgiving kiss,
That make one's life complete.

SATURDAY—DECEMBER 10.

OVER 300 years ago a friend of Brother Lawrence told of a conversation he had with him the first time they met.

"He told me," he wrote, "that in winter, seeing a tree stripped of its leaves, and considering that within a little time the leaves would be renewed and after that the flowers and fruit appear, he received a very high view of the Providence and Power of God which has never since been effaced from his soul."

Or, as Shelley, the poet, put it, perhaps rather more simply, "If winter comes, can spring be far behind?"

A cheering thought for cold, drab winter days!

SUNDAY—DECEMBER 11.

BLESSED are the peacemakers: for they shall be called the children of God.

MONDAY—DECEMBER 12.

THE Lady of the House is a keen knitter.
But you don't need to know about knitting to understand what she told me as her needles clicked away busily the other evening. She said she often thought that knitting was like her life, each row in the pattern representing a simple day. Some rows, like days, go smoothly; others are quite difficult.

"I made a mistake last week," she said. "It would hardly have been noticed so I left it and carried on. But I found I couldn't live with it. In the end I had to rattle it all down and start again."

You can't do that with your life. But you can, learning from your mistakes, give it a new pattern.

EVENING SHADOWS

THE FRIENDSHIP BOOK

TUESDAY—DECEMBER 13.

IT'S nearly Christmas—has he guessed
  The secret for so long concealed?
He's growing fast, it can't be long
  Before the mystery stands revealed.
This year I think he's going to ask—
  It makes me just a little sad—
" Mum, tell me is it really true
  That Santa Claus is only Dad?"

WEDNESDAY—DECEMBER 14.

IN 1940, Gordon McKay from Glasgow was in a Spitfire fighting off German planes over France, when, with his finger on the gun button ready to finish off an already stricken Messerschmidt, he noticed a pair of white baby's bootees hanging in the ME cockpit. Suddenly Gordon saw the pilot not as an enemy but as a father and he lifted his finger from the button. His opponent held up his hand and waved his thanks, and in that fleeting moment Gordon noticed that the German's third finger was missing on his left hand.

In the 1950's, Gordon and his wife and family were on holiday in Bavaria and they fell in with a friendly family from Bremen. Gunther was recounting his wartime experience and said he owed his life to a Spitfire pilot—and that was when Gordon noticed Gunther's left hand and the missing finger . . . .

Not only have the two families become great friends, but in 1980 Gunther's granddaughter was married to Gordon's grandson. I cannot imagine a happier ending to the story—although, of course, it is not an ending but a new beginning.

THE FRIENDSHIP BOOK

WHEN I was a small boy someone wrote this verse in my autograph album. I have never forgotten it:

Do what you can, being what you are,
Shine like a glow-worm if you cannot be a star.
Work like a pulley if you cannot be a crane,
Be a wheel-greaser if you cannot drive the train.

YOU don't perhaps think of the people behind the counter of the Post Office as artists, but here's a little story that shows how wrong you can be.

A German girl went into a city sub-post office towards Christmas with a parcel to post to her handicapped brother near Stuttgart. She asked the man behind the country if he could put on a number of attractive stamps to interest her brother.

A few days later the sender of the parcel had a delighted phone call from her mother in Germany to say that the parcel had arrived. More than that: the wrapping was a real work of art. The man behind the counter had done more than stick on an assortment of stamps.

He had taken the trouble to make an eye-catching design, and the boy in Germany was so taken with it that he was even taking the decorated envelope to bed with him.

It's the small things in life, like that little anonymous act of kindness, that make all the difference, isn't it?

SATURDAY—DECEMBER 17.

PROFESSOR GEDDES MACGREGOR of Los Angeles has written many books, but one of my favourites is the pocket-sized " So Help Me God ", which he describes as " a calendar of quick prayers." Here are just three examples:

" Lord, You hold all things in the hollow of Your hand. Fill the aching hollow in my heart."

" Oh, God, let me not interrupt You with my chatter. Let me listen, rather, to Your still, small voice."

" Oh, God, breathe on me and I shall be refreshed for the morrow."

SUNDAY—DECEMBER 18.

LAY not up for yourselves treasures upon earth, where moth and rust doth corrupt, and where thieves break through and steal.

MONDAY—DECEMBER 19.

HELEN KELLER, blind, deaf and dumb from infancy, wrote in her book, *The World I Live In*: " I have walked with people whose eyes are full of light, but who see nothing in wood, sea or sky, nothing in the city streets, nothing in books. What a witless masquerade is this seeing! It were far better to sail for ever in the night of blindness, with sense and feeling and mind, than to be thus content with the mere act of seeing. They have the sunset, the morning skies, the purple distant hills, yet their souls voyage through this enchanted world with a barren state."

How much more Helen Keller " saw " without sight than some of us see with our eyes!

INGENIOUS

A web of delicate grace,
   Delightful to the eye,
Hands poised in space
   —To catch a fly.
The moral to be drawn is neat:
Even great artists need to eat!

TUESDAY—DECEMBER 20.

YOU feel you're of no importance? You don't count for much? Take heart from these words of Edith Wharton: " There are two ways of spreading light: to be the candle, or the mirror that reflects it."

Either way you can spread a lot of light.

WEDNESDAY—DECEMBER 21.

DR FREDERIC LOOMIS was sitting in the hospital auditorium listening to the Christmas concert. Twenty nurses walked slowly past singing " Silent night! Holy night!" to the accompaniment of three young musicians, one on her harp, another on her cello, the third on her violin.

Afterwards, the harpist approached the doctor. " I don't suppose you recognise me?" she asked. " Do you remember a little girl born with only one good leg?"

Seventeen years rolled back, and Dr Loomis was back in the delivery room, battling with his conscience.

He had often regretted his decision to allow that malformed child to live—but now he spoke to a perfectly healthy young woman: " Go back to your harp for a moment, please, and play ' Silent night ' for me alone. I have a load on my shoulders that no one has ever seen, a load that only you can take away."

As the last strains of " Silent night " faded away, Dr Frederic Loomis found the peace and comfort for which he had waited so long—and a deep gratitude that he had not, after all, betrayed his medical trust.

THE FRIENDSHIP BOOK

WE live in an age where the scientist is able to tell us more and more about the cosmos. We're given facts and figures and photos which truly astound and set one's head in a whirl. For simple-minded folk like me it is all just too vast to comprehend. So I switch off.

Then Christmas approaches and the meaning of life is made clear in the simplest, loveliest way possible. A new baby in a country manger brings the gospel of peace for the redemption of mankind. That's the sort of language I understand, and each year at this time my faith is rekindled.

IN her novel, *I, Judas* Taylor Caldwell makes one of her characters, Gamaliel, a wise member of the Jewish Council, say, " I judge a man not by what he says or does but by what he wants."

Reading that reminded me of a story which Lord Grey of Falloden used to delight in telling. It concerned " a man whom others called poor but who had enough to support himself going about the country in the simplest way, enjoying the life and beauty of it."

This man was once in the company of a millionaire who devoted himself to getting richer and richer. The poor man said to him, " I am a richer man than you are."

" How do you make that out?" demanded the millionaire.

" Well," was the reply, " I have got as much money as I want—and you haven't!"

How rich and happy we are when we learn the secret of contentment.

SATURDAY—DECEMBER 24.

> *I THINK of Christmas long ago,*
> *The snow, the lights, the holly,*
> *Departed friends we used to know,*
> *Of days carefree and jolly.*
> *And yet my heart's from sadness free,*
> *I hear the bells' sweet ringing,*
> *And clear and clearer comes to me*
> *The message that they're bringing.*

SUNDAY—DECEMBER 25.

AND she brought forth her first-born son, and wrapped him in swaddling clothes, and laid him in a manger.

MONDAY—DECEMBER 26.

JUST before Christmas, the Lady of the House and I visited our old friend Mary to take her a little gift and our Christmas greetings.

" Are you all ready for Christmas, Mary?" the Lady of the House asked, looking at the Christmas tree, the holly, mistletoe and other decorations, and the pile of presents by the tree.

" Well, nearly," said Mary. " The pudding and the mince pies and all that sort of thing are ready, but there is still one thing I have to do, and I am never quite sure whether I should do it right at the beginning or leave it till now."

We looked round, trying to spot the omission. Then Mary rose and took down her Bible. " I feel I'm never really ready for Christmas until I have read all about it again in the Gospels."

Mary knows the true meaning of " getting ready for Christmas."

HOMECOMING

TUESDAY—DECEMBER 27.

EACH day's a new beginning,
So start it with a smile;
Enjoy the art of living,
Do things that are worthwhile,
Like loving and forgiving,
And having time to spare,
To make some person happy,
By showing that you care.

WEDNESDAY—DECEMBER 28.

SUCCESS in public life brings all kinds of temptations that are often very hard to resist. One famous man whose happy family life was the envy of his friends was asked how he did it.

He answered: " If you can find the courage to be yourself, to be the person God intended you to be, you'll come out all right."

It's not always easy to refuse to go along with the crowd. It takes a special brand of courage to keep true to yourself and dare to be different. But don't we all have to do it from time to time? Look in the right direction and we'll " come out all right."

THURSDAY—DECEMBER 29.

WHAT a lot we take for granted! When Carl Linnaeus, the great Swedish botanist, visited England, he saw, for the first time in his life, a gorse bush in full flower. It is said that he was so overwhelmed by its beauty that he instantly knelt before it, giving thanks to God.

Let us open our eyes and our hearts today and look at the wonders around us as for the first time.

THE FRIENDSHIP BOOK

IN the well-known television programme, " This Is Your Life ", the subject is presented with a book recording his life. It is an appropriate symbol. The Biblical psalmist speaks of our life as " a tale that is told ", and the 17th century writer, Richard Gove, has a passage in which he compares man to a book:

" His birth is the title page; his baptism the preface; his youth the table of contents; his life the body of the volume; his blunders the errata and his repentance the correction of them. Men, like books, are large and small, quartos, folios and tiny volumes. Some are fairer bound than others, and some that lack in show make up in durability of binding and in the value of their contents. Some are pious and some profane, some full of wisdom and some full of folly, but each must have a final page with the word ' Finis '."

A quaint fancy, perhaps, yet we might well take heed what we write in our life's record today!

IN some country districts of Scotland farmers still take their guns and fire them into the air to " shoot the Old Year out."

Of course, there are things we shall want to remember gratefully about the year that has gone and it is right that we should. But, as for the rest, as Shakespeare said, " Let's not burden our remembrance with a heaviness that's gone." Shoot it!

May our outlook be that of St Paul . . . " Forgetting those things which are behind, and reaching forth unto those things which are before."

Where the Photographs were taken

MAJESTY — *Eshaness, Shetland.*
RIDING OUT — *Epping Forest, Essex.*
UNFORGETTABLE — *Bognor, Sussex.*
EVER NEW — *Strand on the Green, Middlesex.*
WOODLANDS — *near Rockford, North Devon.*
BRAVE SHOW — *Edinburgh Castle.*
JOURNEY'S END — *Chilham, Kent.*
OLD FRIEND — *Moniaive, Dumfriesshire.*
HEALING — *Falls of Falloch, near Crianlarich, Perthshire.*
COUNTRY JOY — *River Avon, Hampshire.*
HEAVENWARDS — *Norwich Cathedral, Norfolk.*
OASIS — *Lincoln's Inn, London.*
AT EASE — *Valley Gardens, Harrogate, Yorkshire.*
THE WANDERERS — *Loch Lomond, Dunbartonshire/
Stirlingshire.*
CHERISHED — *White Cragg Gardens, Langdale, Cumbria.*
AROUND US — *Mellerstain, Berwickshire.*
DREAMLAND — *Llanrhaiadr, Clwyd.*
RENEWAL — *Colne, Wiltshire.*
EVENING SHADOWS — *Troutbeck, Cumbria.*
HOMECOMING — *Helensburgh, Dunbartonshire.*

Printed and Published by D. C. Thomson & Co. Ltd.,
185 Fleet Street, London EC4A 2HS.
© D. C. Thomson & Co. Ltd., 1982.
ISBN 0 85116 267 3